ATTORNEY FEE HU$TLE

A CONSUMER'S GUIDE TO DISPUTING LEGAL FEES

ATTORNEY FEE HU$TLE

ISBN (Paperback): 979-8-218-83373-2

For a full legal disclaimer, please see the following page.

Printed in the United States of America.
First Edition.

Published by **Attorney Fee Hustle**
Website: **attorneyfeehustle.com**

Legal Disclaimer

This book is for informational and educational purposes only. It is not legal advice. The material presented here is not a substitute for obtaining legal advice from a licensed attorney who can evaluate your specific circumstances. Laws, rules, ethical standards, and court procedures vary by jurisdiction and may change over time. Reading this book does not create an attorney–client relationship. The author is not acting as an attorney for any reader and cannot provide legal advice, representation, or individualized guidance. Examples, case summaries, and illustrations are provided solely to explain general concepts and should not be interpreted as predictions of outcome or statements about how any court or agency will rule in a particular case. Although every effort has been made to ensure the accuracy of the information provided, the author makes no warranties or guarantees, express or implied, regarding the content of this book or its applicability to any reader's situation. The author and publisher disclaim all liability for any loss, damage, or adverse consequences resulting from the use or misuse of the information contained herein. If you believe you have a legal problem or need advice about an attorney's conduct or billing practices, you should consult a qualified attorney, your state bar association, or another appropriate authority for assistance.

The goal of education is the advancement of knowledge and the dissemination of truth.

John F. Kennedy

AUTHOR NOTES

You do not need a law degree to challenge unreasonable attorney fees. This guide provides resources to help you decode questionable billing practices that can lead to unfair legal bills. By recognizing these practices, you can effectively dispute inaccurate or excessive charges. As a practical matter, you have the right to question fees on your invoice because of an attorney's professional rules of conduct. When you dispute problematic legal fees, the burden shifts to the attorney to justify the amounts charged. You should not be responsible for additional costs simply to ensure that an attorney fulfills their fiduciary duty of accountability.

A dramatic increase in the number of lawyers and law firms in the United States began in the 1970s and continued throughout the 1990s. This shift in the legal landscape, along with a 1975 U. S. Supreme Court ruling,[1] paved the way for billing by the hour, the focus of this guide. Currently, hourly billing, a notoriously subjective form of invoicing, predominates in most legal sectors. In fact, a recent survey shows that about 97% of law firms now offer hourly rates.[2]

The practice of law is a noble profession. However, it can also be a business driven by profit. And profit motives can compromise an attorney's fiduciary duty to act in a client's best interests. For this reason, it would be prudent for clients to take a proactive approach in monitoring their legal fees to ensure compliance with the legal profession's code of ethics. As law firms increasingly turn to AI to support their billing rates,[3] clients need all the help they can get to ensure they receive fair legal bills.

Although I no longer practice law, I understand the business of practicing law. Drawing on corporate, academic, and legal experience, I have spent over a decade researching attorney billing practices. This work has resulted in a user-friendly resource that offers practical tools to help clients analyze their attorney’s invoices and develop strategies to dispute unreasonable fees. This guide includes a comprehensive discussion of questionable billing practices, supported by references to case law, legal journals, law review articles, legal textbooks, and state bar associations.

In Chapter 11, I've added a commentary on my experiences from both sides of the bar to explain the motivation for writing this book. My legal experiences have been good and bad. Still, I have never lost sight of the importance of responsible behavior for both lawyers and clients. I also came away with a very important lesson: transparent billing not only upholds an attorney's high standards but also maintains a client's trust. While most attorneys adhere to their ethical duties, this book focuses on those who have forgotten their commitment to conduct themselves with honesty, civility, and integrity.

---

1. *Goldfarb v. Virginia State Bar*, 421 U.S. 773 (1975).

2. Clio, *2023 Legal Trends Report* (2023).

3. *J.G. v. NYC Department of Education*, 23 Civ. 959 (SDNY 2024).

CONTENTS

PREFACE

If an attorney intentionally overbills their client, isn't that fraud?

A divorce attorney exaggerates the hours spent drafting a simple motion. An appellate attorney overstates the time allocated to research. A civil attorney charges for a half-hour conference after meeting with a client for only 15 minutes. A bankruptcy attorney submits an invoice claiming 60 hours of work in a single day.

When faced with legal worries for the first time, you may have little insight into how bill-padding occurs or why unreasonable fees are tolerated. The practices noted above violated the attorney's code of ethics. Yet where is the public outrage?

With hourly rates ranging from $100 to over $1,000, intentional overbilling can quickly inflate an attorney's invoice. According to an article in the American Bar Association Journal, a survey found that 21% of lawyers "upbilled" by rounding up their hours worked to the next hour or half hour.[1]

This guide aims to support clients who have had the unfortunate experience of working with attorneys who fail to uphold the high ethical standards of the legal profession.

Intentional overbilling not only damages a client's finances but can also weaken public confidence in the legal system. As a client, you may be unaware of these improper tactics or fear the stress, financial burden, and potential backlash from your attorney if you decide to dispute your legal fees.

However, a little knowledge can go a long way in helping you monitor your legal bills. The perception that padding legal bills is just business as usual must be addressed. An attorney who billed 90 hours in one day believed that his fees were not problematic, as he claimed that everybody did it. Another attorney who was sanctioned for charging excessive fees explained that she only did "what I saw everybody else doing."[2]

Of course, not every attorney charges unreasonable fees, but those who do should be held accountable.

If you decide to dispute your attorney's invoice, you may want to avoid the added expense of hiring an expert or retaining a second attorney to question suspected overbilling. Fortunately, no-cost alternatives are available. This guide aims to reshape public perception of how to effectively challenge excessive legal fees.

This guide will help you to identify, document, and challenge unreasonable legal fees. It includes educational resources to help you evaluate billing charges and prepare for a straightforward discussion with your attorney—or, as a last resort, legal action.

HERE IS A QUICK LOOK AT WHAT'S INSIDE:

Choose Your Attorney Wisely
Before hiring an attorney, take some time for research and make an informed decision. Check for on-line reviews, ask for recommendations, and consider the attorney's experience and reputation.

Understand Fee Agreements and Retainers
Familiarize yourself with the various types of fee agreements, including hourly, flat, contingency, and Alternative Fee Arrangements. (AFA) Obtain a written contract that clearly outlines the attorney's billing practices and rates. Recognize the different kinds of advances (retainers) and request clarification of terms you don't understand.

Identify Problematic fees
As soon as you receive your invoice, review it carefully. Look for red flags such as vague descriptions of the legal work performed, block billing, and excessive charges for clerical work. This guide explains 18 of the most common examples of bill padding.

Document Questions with a Fee Audit
After identifying potentially excessive fees, document each charge with a brief explanation for your attorney's review. Compile the questionable fees into an audit as outlined in this guide.

Maintain Communication
Stay in contact with your attorney. If you don't understand certain charges on your invoice, ask questions and request a more detailed explanation. Send a written request if a phone call to your attorney's office doesn't give you the information you need.

Challenge Excessive Fees

Do not hesitate to challenge fees that seem unreasonable. You have the right to question and resolve problematic legal bills. You have options: a discussion with your attorney, a complaint to the State Bar, Mediation, Arbitration or a Legal Malpractice lawsuit. The choice is yours.

Tools and Templates

The resources in this book are designed to help you methodically analyze attorney fees. Templates and checklists are included to support your legal bill review. Chapter 9 includes a QR code linking to a website with updated materials and additional information.

A Companion Website

www.attorneyfeehustle.com offers an interactive resource to supplement this guide. Visitors can submit questions about the book's content and receive clear, practical answers from a real person, not AI. The site does not provide legal advice. Instead, it helps readers better understand legal billing practices and prepare informed questions for their attorneys.

---

1. Weiss, Debra Cassens, "Red-Flag Billing Practices Chronicled; Report Finds 'upbilling' by 21 Percent of Law Firms." *ABA Journal*, March 28, 2017.

2. *Matter of Gendel*, 303 A. 3d 1292, 255 NJ 500, (NJ: Supreme Court, 2023).

Chapter 1

INTRODUCTION

Overbilling: stretching ethical limits or breaking the law?

Attorneys are ethically obligated to charge reasonable fees;[1] however, when they bill by the hour, there may be a temptation to inflate the time billed for the legal services they provide. As a client, you may not be aware of *bill padding,* the unethical practice of overstating the hours an attorney claims to have worked to increase their fees.

Unfortunately, there are numerous ways that bill padding can improperly inflate fees. Examples include churning, block billing, charging for tasks not completed, and using vague billing descriptions. This guide will show you how to identify, document, and challenge questionable charges. You have every right to dispute unreasonable fees to avoid the Attorney Fee Hu$tle.

However, disputing legal fees is not easy. The thought of challenging an attorney can be stressful. Clients understandably feel intimidated by the idea of confronting the very professionals they trusted to represent them. This book aims to change that way of thinking. Step by step, you will be guided through the process of effectively disputing excessive fees without incurring additional expenses, and hopefully, without adding unnecessary stress.

Bill-padding and overbilling are general terms that describe potentially unethical tactics such as block billing, chipping, churning, duplicate billing, inflating hours, high minimum increments, and charging attorney rates for paralegal tasks. These questionable practices, which will be explained in detail in subsequent chapters, are used by some attorneys to overstate the amount billed. You should not have to pay more than what you initially agreed upon. As an unsuspecting client, you may find yourself facing an overwhelming amount of attorney fees that do not match the legal services provided.

Unethical practices can unfairly affect a client in a variety of ways. A fee agreement may contain complex legal language that an average client cannot easily understand. Basic clerical tasks may be billed at a paralegal's rate. Charges for services not performed may be listed amongst reasonable charges on an invoice. A legal expert noted that hourly billing, "...involves such a wide degree of personal discretion, those attempting to cheat may perceive, quite accurately, that the odds of getting caught are close to zero."[2]

Some commentators and court rulings have noted that questionable billing practices are merely pushing ethical boundaries or have been downplayed as poor timekeeping. A senior columnist for a legal magazine opined, "For whatever reason, I can't sum up the outrage that some members of the profession are expressing over the lawyer who padded his billables." She also stated, "[T]here's a sense that padding billables is a victimless crime."[3] Yet billing a client for legal services not performed crosses an ethical line. As a law professor stated, "Intentional over-billing a client is a form of theft."[4]

In a disciplinary decision, a State Board found that an attorney "deliberately increased the hours billed in order to charge a premium that he was not entitled to"[5] but an Appellate Court concluded that his actions amounted to only negligent conduct.

A more serious case concerns an attorney who, over 40 years, received more than 200 disciplinary complaints, including approximately 120 allegations related to client trust account matters. Even so, he was not publicly disciplined by the state bar until his disbarment in 2022.[6] Prospective clients likely had limited access to information about his complaint history or the potential risks associated with retaining his services. It's worth remembering that under the profession's ethical rules, an attorney commits misconduct when they "engage in conduct involving dishonesty, fraud, deceit, or misrepresentation."[7]

If concerns about an attorney's questionable practices are not adequately addressed, clients may face significant obstacles in resolving disputes. A major problem with unethical billing practices is the lack of *detailed* information available to individual clients concerned about their fees. The public rarely hears about lawyers overbilling individual clients because fee disputes are often resolved through confidential, out-of-court settlements, making it difficult to research an attorney's past practices. Although articles concerning attorneys violating their ethical obligations are published, they are often found in legal subscriber databases that can only be accessed for a fee.

To effectively dispute unreasonable legal fees, you must first understand *how* attorneys pad their bills.

"Most dishonest billing is the perfect crime," Professor William G. Ross explains in his book, *The Honest Hour*, "because there is no practical manner of verifying the accuracy of most time records."[8] However, if a client can identify and document potential overbilling based on the legal profession's ethical obligations, the burden shifts to the attorney to substantiate those fees.

Chapters 4 and 5 describe eighteen common bill-padding practices and demonstrate how each practice can be used to inflate legal fees. These chapters will help you learn to identify problematic billing entries. And by closely monitoring your attorney's invoices, you will be able to recognize charges that may not accurately reflect the work performed.

For example, if a client questions a $200 fee charged by a paralegal for copying a file, it becomes the attorney's responsibility to justify why a paralegal performed this typically non-billable clerical task and why it was billed at a paralegal's rate. A federal court decision clarified this issue by stating the "burden of proof is on the attorney to establish the value of his services."[9]

Determining the validity of your attorney's fees may require effort, but the time spent will undoubtedly be worthwhile.

Once you understand the extent of your attorney's invoicing errors, this book will explain how to create an audit of your legal fees. The results can provide useful information to your attorney, a state bar organization, a mediator, an arbitrator, or even help you prepare for a legal malpractice lawsuit. You'll find more details about each option in later chapters. One legal authority has suggested, "It is practically impossible to eliminate overbilling."[10] So it will be up to you to learn the techniques necessary to detect excessive charges in your case.

Every fee dispute should begin with a direct conversation with your attorney. However, if your conversation is not productive, and your fee issues remain unresolved, you have options. Chapters 7 and 8 explain the steps to take if your attorney will not address your concerns.

This book is intended for individual clients who may lack the resources or negotiating power to effectively challenge their legal fees. Most of the information written about attorney fees and relevant case law has focused on corporate and governmental billing issues with law firms, primarily due to the substantial costs involved in civil lawsuits and insurance claims. Corporations have used legal bill audits for years to manage their legal expenses and often hire independent legal auditors to review their attorney fees. "One legal auditor estimated 85% of his audits revealed billing for work product that cannot be located, too many lawyers at conferences or depositions, and vague time entries such as review file."[11]

By identifying and reducing excessive claims for attorney fees and expenses, corporate legal fee audits can lead to significant savings. Until now, individual clients may not have been aware that they can access similar safeguards.

The following chapters outline practical methods to protect clients from unreasonable legal fees. A parent involved in a contentious custody battle is one example of a client who may need help in evaluating the accuracy of their invoices. I have seen cases where individuals have spent their life savings amid the emotional turmoil of divorce proceedings. Family law litigants were expected to spend an estimated $13.2 billion on legal fees in 2024.[12] The likelihood that even a small percentage of those fees is unreasonable provides a valid argument to protect yourself against excessive fees.

Another area of concern is probate law, where unconscionable attorney fees can needlessly reduce your inheritance if you are not vigilant. Likewise, in civil lawsuits where attorneys bill by the hour, you may face improper fees for simple clerical tasks.

Truthfully, disputing attorney fees is often difficult. Attorneys can be intimidating, and even if you suspect overbilling, you might be afraid to address the issue because of the fear of losing representation. We often hire attorneys during highly emotional times and look to them as our saviors. But we may forget that they are also a business.

However, if an attorney intentionally pads their bills, they violate their fiduciary duty by allowing their profit motives to conflict with your legal interests. In contrast, a reputable attorney will want to promptly resolve potential fee issues so they can focus on your case. Whether you're a family court litigant or an insurance company fighting a million-dollar fee request, the principle remains the same: Attorneys cannot ethically charge unconscionable fees. "Hours that are not properly billed to one's client also are not properly billed to one's adversary pursuant to statutory authority."[13]

You have a right to reasonable attorney fees—and now you have a cost-effective guide to identify, document, and challenge legal bills. *Attorney Fee Hu$tle* changes the narrative. This guide will walk you through the steps of analyzing legal invoices to prepare a detailed fee audit for effectively disputing excessive fees. With this support, you will be able to shift the burden to the attorney to prove that their fees are reasonable according to their Professional Rules of Conduct.

1. American Bar Association, "Rule 1.5: Fees," in Model Rules of Professional Conduct, 2020.
2. Lerman, Lisa, "Regulation of Unethical Billing Practices: Progress and Prospects," *The Professional Lawyer*, 1998, 90–97.
3. Chen, Vivia, "The US Overbilling Scandal: Why We Should Not Be So Shocked," *Law.Com International*, January 24, 2019.
4. Packel, Dan, "Lawyers Caught Overbilling? The Billable Hour Shares the Blame," *The American Lawyer*, January 18, 2019.
5. *In re Romansky*, 938 A.2d 733,743 (D.C. 2007).
6. www.calbar.ca.gov/Portals/0/documents/Open-Letter-Girardi-Disclosure-11-03-22.pdf
7. American Bar Association, "Rule 8.4: Misconduct" in Model Rules of Professional Conduct, 2020.
8. Ross, William G., *The Honest Hour: The Ethics of Time-Based Billing by Attorneys* (Durham, N.C: Carolina Academic Press, 1996).
9. *Dobbs v. DePuy Orthopedics, Inc.*, 842 F.3d 1045 (7th Cir. 2016).
10. Richmond, Douglas R., "For a Few Dollars More: The Perplexing Problem of Unethical Billing Practices by Lawyers," *South Carolina Law Review* 60, no. 1 (2008): 63–121.
11. Ricker, Darlene "Greed, Ignorance, and Overbilling: Some Lawyers Have Given New Meaning to the Term 'Legal Fiction,'" *ABA Journal* 80, no. 8 (1994): 62–66.
12. Diment, Dmitry, *Family Law & Divorce Lawyers & Attorneys in the US*, IBISWorld. November 2024.
13. *Copeland v. Marshall*, 641 F.2d 880, 891 (D.C. Cir. 1980).

CHAPTER 2

TEN TIPS TO AVOID UNREASONABLE LEGAL FEES

Manage and control your attorney fees!

This chapter outlines *proactive* steps to help you avoid problematic fees, especially if you are hiring an attorney for the first time. You'll find suggestions on selecting the right attorney, strategies to prevent future disputes, and practical tips for monitoring legal bills. This chapter also provides an overview of the dispute process and introduces 18 common bill-padding practices that will be discussed throughout this guide.

TEN STEPS TO PROTECT YOURSELF AGAINST EXCESSIVE LEGAL FEES

1. Choose your attorney wisely
2. Collect your documents
3. Read and question the fee agreement
4. Do not sign the fee agreement in the office
5. Think twice before calling your attorney
6. Start a telephone log
7. Promptly review each invoice
8. Identify and document potential bill-padding
9. Communicate with your attorney
10. Challenge excessive attorney fees

1. CHOOSE YOUR ATTORNEY WISELY

The national average cost for a contested divorce exceeds $10,000. Doesn't it make sense to research your attorney before committing to a relationship that may last for months or, if you're unlucky, years? The attorney you choose will have access to sensitive personal information and will play a significant role in important legal decisions. The selection process for an attorney typically begins with an initial consultation and ends with a written fee agreement. The agreement should finalize in writing the financial responsibilities and obligations for both you and your attorney, including the type of retainer required for your case. This chapter introduces you to consultations, fee agreements, and retainers, while subsequent chapters provide more detailed information on these topics.

Talk to people you know.
Although each case is different, a personal referral can serve as a starting point. Contact a neighbor, relative, or trusted friend who may be able to suggest an attorney. Call the local bar association for recommendations. Look up the attorney's history with the State Bar Association. Check online. Google, Avvo, Yelp, and the Better Business Bureau are all sources of information.

However, be cautious: if a client loses in court, they may express frustration in online reviews rather than acknowledging the underlying challenges of their case. If you have time, consider attending a hearing to observe how your prospective attorney conducts themselves in court.

Choose a lawyer with experience.
Look for lawyers with expertise in the relevant field of law. Some states have certified specialists with additional experience and educational requirements that earn them a title and, of course, the ability to charge a higher fee. However, the most expensive attorney is not necessarily the best choice. In some cities, $500 an hour has become the new normal. Imagine the costs if your case goes to trial; billed hours can multiply quickly. Be cautious about paying a premium simply because you are upset. The attorney with the highest hourly rate is not necessarily the best choice.

Select an attorney who listens to your concerns and respects your objectives.

For instance, if you prefer a joint custody arrangement, avoid attorneys who encourage avoidable disputes or unreasonable financial demands. Keep in mind that prolonged and needless conflict can increase legal costs.

Ask questions and carefully consider the attorney's responses. Did the attorney treat you with respect? Were your questions answered clearly? Did you receive enough information to make an informed decision?

Choose an attorney based on your research and not your emotions.

After I was formally served with divorce papers, I felt angry and hurt. I asked an acquaintance to recommend a tough divorce attorney. Based on her suggestion, I made an appointment and quickly signed a fee agreement. As we prepared for a settlement conference, a member of the attorney's staff mentioned that another client's former husband had recently taken his own life after a similar conference. I must admit that comment gave me pause.

I soon ended the relationship with the attorney. The initial settlement conference was unproductive, and I became increasingly concerned about the firm's billing practices. Although I was initially impressed by the attorney's reputation, my legal fees escalated rapidly with no end in sight. I had signed over my future pension payments as collateral to hire this attorney, and soon realized I was digging myself into a deep financial hole. On a positive note, the experience motivated me to apply to law school.

Consultations

A legal consultation is usually the first meeting with an attorney during your search for legal representation. An attorney may provide a free consultation or request a one-time payment. The purpose of the consultation is twofold: for you to provide the facts surrounding your legal issue to the attorney and for the attorney to decide if they are able and willing to take your case. After discussing your legal matter, the attorney should explain the required retainer, the billing rates, potential expenses, and the services to be performed. Try meeting with several attorneys to determine if your personalities and legal objectives match.

Free You may have seen attorney advertisements for a "free half-hour consultation." Some attorneys offer free consultations to get prospective clients in the door to determine if your case is worth their time. The consultation may consist of an in-person visit to the attorney's office or an online submission of your legal issues, which will be forwarded to the attorney's office for review. An attorney is taking a calculated risk because there is no guarantee that the time spent on this free consultation will result in a new client. Yet for the client, initial consultations without the consequences of a formal fee agreement are an effective way to evaluate the attorney and the feasibility of the case.

Fee Paid Attorneys can also require payment for their initial consultation to ensure you are serious about seeking legal advice. The fee-paid consultation typically requires payment prior to the meeting. Herein lies the first example of competing goals between you and an attorney.

Your cost-efficient plan for finding the right lawyer may conflict with a lawyer's objective of being compensated for every hour they work. However, since the one-time payment for a consultation covers a defined and limited meeting, there should be no exposure to unforeseen charges.

It's common to view an attorney as your champion who will solve all your problems, but consider the potential costs involved. Take the time to compare options before making an informed decision. Give yourself an opportunity to talk with more than one lawyer. Numerous published articles and books offer valuable insights on selecting the right attorney. A quick internet search will provide you with multiple resources. The key point to remember is to take your time and research several different attorneys.

After you have completed your research and decided upon an attorney, they should provide you with a formal written agreement. Carefully review and sign this agreement before the attorney begins working on your case. The details of this legal contract, including the type of advance payment (retainer) involved, will be discussed in the next chapter.

2. COLLECT YOUR DOCUMENTS

Prepare for your initial meeting with your prospective attorney. During litigation, you may need to make critical financial decisions. Gather all relevant paperwork and supporting documentation to have on hand as needed. Organizing this information and having it readily available will be more cost-effective than relying on your attorney to collect the data.

3. READ AND QUESTION THE FEE AGREEMENT

Know that you begin at a disadvantage.

A fee agreement is a contract drafted by someone with years of experience preparing legal documents. If you come across unfamiliar terms, don't hesitate to contact the attorney's office and ask for an explanation. Better yet, ask the attorney to walk you through the agreement before you sign it. When attorneys bill by the hour, it's important to understand their billing practices so you can avoid paying for charges that may not accurately reflect the services performed.

Thoroughly review your fee agreement.

Don't skim through the document; read it closely, page by page. This is where the financial relationship with your attorney *should be* spelled out, and missing the fine print can lead to costly misunderstandings. One client didn't realize her agreement left out the hourly rates for the firm's staff. When her first invoice arrived, she received a shocking and expensive surprise.

Read the language of the agreement carefully.

It may include a lien provision stating that the attorney is entitled to collect payment from funds recovered on your behalf. Attorney associations often recommend including such liens to protect an attorney's right to collect unpaid fees. In some jurisdictions, the attorney may be required to advise the prospective client in writing to seek independent counsel before agreeing to the lien.

Decide if you want to pay a second attorney to review the first attorney's agreement before signing. It's understandable that fee agreements can feel frustrating or intimidating.

Liens, nonrefundable retainers, engagement fees, and mandatory binding arbitration for all disputes are a few examples of limiting terms that you may find in your fee agreement. Attorneys often use these conditions to secure payment for their services, but at a cost. You might not fully understand that you are waiving certain rights. When signing the fee agreement, take your time to review the terms carefully. If there is anything that you don't understand, don't hesitate to ask your attorney for an explanation. Fee agreements are discussed in more detail in the next chapter.

4. DON'T SIGN THE FEE AGREEMENT IN THEIR OFFICE

Once you have talked to several people and researched your prospective attorney's background, you may have decided on your attorney. They may be the third attorney you've consulted, and you feel comfortable with their attitude and commitment to your case. You are in their office, and it's time to sign the retainer or fee agreement. All too often, you will be emotionally distracted because you hope this attorney will be a solution to all your problems.

You may be tempted to sign a contract to relieve the weight of litigation. But be careful: Your fee agreement can significantly affect your case and wallet. Ask to take the fee agreement home so you can read it thoroughly. If the attorney hesitates to let you do so and does not provide an adequate explanation, you may wish to reconsider moving forward. An attorney may try to persuade you with tales of recent case victories. Be cautious about relying solely on promotional claims or prior success stories. Remember, every case is unique, and the substantial proceeds obtained for a previous client may have no relevance to the facts in your case.

5. THINK TWICE BEFORE YOU CALL YOUR ATTORNEY

Your attorney is not a therapist. All too often, distraught clients will call their attorney and vent about the opposing party's actions. These phone calls may be unnecessary from a legal perspective and could be better handled by support staff. Demanding to talk to your attorney about non-legal matters can take time away from the genuine issues in your case. In one reviewed invoice, the vast majority of a client's monthly fees consisted of charges for non-essential phone calls. Before you pick up the phone to call your attorney's office, ask yourself these questions:

Is this a legal question that requires immediate attention?

Am I calling for legal advice or to complain about the other party?

If the attorney answers my question, will it solve my problem?

What do I expect will happen after the phone call?

If your questions do not require immediate attention from the attorney, compile them into a single list. This will save time and help ensure that all your concerns are addressed during a subsequent phone call or meeting.

6. START A TELEPHONE LOG

One simple notebook can save you hundreds of dollars in fees. All you need to do is record the time you spend talking with your attorney or their staff on the phone. Be sure to identify the person you are speaking with and note the time of the conversation. A sample entry might look like this:

10:00 a.m. to 10:03 a.m. I spoke with my attorney's paralegal about setting up a conference with the attorney.

Remember, your attorney's office does the same thing except the attorney and their staff charge for phone calls and bill for increments of their time at rates of hundreds of dollars per hour. Doesn't it make sense to be proactive and write down the timing of all your phone calls? Subsequently, when you receive your attorney's invoice, you can compare your notes to the amounts charged on your invoice and identify any discrepancies.

The minimum hourly increment charged by an attorney's office is an important detail in hourly billing, especially regarding telephone calls. Chapter 4 offers a more detailed discussion of this practice; the following is a brief example. A fee agreement may state that the attorney can charge a minimum of 0.25 hours (15 minutes) for a task, regardless of the actual time spent. This means that if your attorney charges $500 an hour and spends five minutes on a phone call with you, the fee agreement allows them to bill you for the full 15 minutes: $125.

In reality, five minutes of actual work amounted to $41.66, but there is an *additional* $83.34 billed for ten minutes of unspecified services. While attorneys may explain that this practice is permissible under their fee agreements, it can raise legitimate billing concerns for clients.

Keeping a telephone log is a simple way to protect yourself. By tracking the actual time spent on calls with your attorney, you can compare your records to their invoices and identify any issues. If an attorney genuinely needs to prepare for a phone call, accurate descriptions of the work performed are more useful than recording time entries without a clear explanation.

7. PROMPTLY REVIEW EACH INVOICE

Once you have researched your attorney and signed the fee agreement, the next step is to thoroughly review your first invoice. It is essential to analyze your invoice promptly, as any delays could lead to significant problems in the event of a future fee dispute. If you do not raise concerns immediately, your attorney may argue that your silence amounts to acceptance of the charges. In fee disputes, attorneys can attempt to defend their invoices by claiming, "You didn't complain when you received the bill," or "The charges only became an issue after you lost your case."

Your fee agreement might even include a clause stating that fees are presumed valid unless you object within a specified time frame.

In some cases, courts have held that if a client fails to raise a timely and specific objection to an invoice, their silence may be interpreted as acceptance of the charges.[1]

Using the information in this book, you will be able to ask informed questions about suspected billing errors. By being proactive, you can protect yourself from unreasonable fees. It's much easier to question fees *before* you pay your invoice than to request a refund later.

8. IDENTIFY AND DOCUMENT POTENTIAL BILL-PADDING

Your attorney has an ethical duty to charge reasonable fees,[2] and you have the right to know how those fees are calculated. A legal invoice should not be a complicated puzzle or a source of questionable billing that quietly inflates costs. Recognizing these practices is essential to protecting yourself from excessive legal bills. To help you get started, listed below are the most common bill-padding tactics you'll learn to recognize throughout this book.

1. **A lack of detail in describing an attorney's charges**
2. **A lack of detail in describing staff charges**
3. **Billing expenses above cost**
4. **Billing for tasks not performed**
5. **Block billing**
6. **Charges for clerical tasks billed by a paralegal**
7. **Charges for paralegal tasks billed by an attorney**
8. **Charges related to billing questions**
9. **Chipping**
10. **Churning**

11. Duplicate billing
12. Excessive entries for document review
13. Excessive legal research
14. Excessive time to complete a task
15. Fees not in compliance with the fee agreement
16. High minimum increments
17. The overuse of "rounded" time estimates
18. Vague descriptions

Once you have identified the questionable fees on your invoice, this guide will help you prepare an audit that lays out the specific problematic charges and explains the reason for each dispute.

9. COMMUNICATE WITH YOUR ATTORNEY

Attorneys are human, and like anyone else, they can make honest mistakes. Still, it's natural to feel uneasy about questioning the charges on your invoice. A reputable attorney will take your concerns seriously and work quickly to resolve them so that both of you can stay focused on the main issues in your case. In contrast, some attorneys may be less responsive, even when presented with clear documentation.

When you present your audit to an attorney, you are offering an organized record of the fees you are questioning, along with the reasons for your concerns. If an attorney refuses to address your valid billing issues, it may be time to reassess the working relationship.

10. DON'T BE AFRAID TO CHALLENGE YOUR ATTORNEY'S FEES

If you are unable to resolve a fee dispute directly with your attorney, you still have additional options. Unreasonable fees may be challenged through a State Bar complaint, mediation, arbitration, or a civil lawsuit.

When you add questionable attorney fees to an already stressful legal matter, the pressure can become overwhelming. You might be caught in a dispute over custody or the division of your marital property, while your legal bills continue to climb. Or you may be watching your inheritance dwindle because an executor is approving excessive fees. Both situations can place a significant financial strain on a client.

Unfortunately, clients may find it easier to downplay the consequences of bill padding by convincing themselves that unreasonable fees are simply part of the process. In doing so, they fail to consider the possibility that their attorney is not effectively managing their case. A lawyer's professionalism isn't limited to the courtroom; it's also reflected in how they run their practice. After all, you are their business.

Once you have retained an attorney, focus on building a relationship where you feel comfortable asking questions about potentially excessive charges or confusing legal terms. You have every right to protect your interests and expect accountability.

---

1. *Shaw v. Silver*, 95 AD 3d 416 - NY: Appellate Div., 1st Dept. 2012; *Law Off. Of Mark S. Helweil v. Karambelas,* 2019 NY Slip Op 32308 - NY: Supreme Court 2019; *Schlenker v. Cascino,* 2012 NY Slip Op 33066 - NY: Supreme Court, Albany 2012.

2. American Bar Association, "Rule 1.5: Fees," in Model Rules of Professional Conduct, 2020.

CHAPTER 3

FEE AGREEMENTS AND RETAINERS

Lawyers have an ethical duty to charge reasonable fees.

To protect yourself from problematic fees and expensive disputes, it is important to understand the simple principle that governs every attorney's billing practices: "A lawyer shall not make an agreement or charge or collect an unreasonable fee."[1] This principle, reflected in the legal profession's code of conduct, supports a client's ability to challenge fees that seem unfair. A well-drafted fee agreement generally reflects this rule by defining the scope of legal services to be provided and the potential costs involved. Understanding fee agreements is the first step in effectively managing your attorney fees.

This chapter begins with a checklist of key legal and contractual terms that are essential for understanding your fee agreement.

FEE AGREEMENT CHECKLIST

Read through your attorney's fee agreement carefully before you sign it. A written agreement protects you and your attorney, reduces misunderstandings, and helps prevent unreasonable fees.

General Requirements

-Do I have a written fee agreement?
-Is the scope of representation clearly stated?
-Does the agreement specify the amount of retainer?
-Is there an explanation for termination?
-Have I received a copy signed by both parties?

Retainers

-Is the type of retainer clearly explained?
-For deposits: Will unused funds be returned to me?
-Will the retainer be placed in a client trust account?
-What happens when my original retainer is exhausted?
-Can the attorney withdraw funds without prior notice?

Billing Method

-Is the billing method identified?
-For hourly billing: Are attorney and staff rates listed?
-Are billing increments specified?
-For flat fee: Is the exact scope of work described in writing?
-For contingency: Is the percentage fee stated?
-Are potential expenses outlined?
-Can billing rates increase during the representation?

-How frequently will I receive itemized invoices?
-Am I charged for administrative or clerical tasks?
-Are interest charges or late fees disclosed?

Key Terms to Review
-Does the agreement contain an arbitration clause?
-Is the arbitration binding or non-binding ?
-Is there a deadline to dispute charges on invoices?
-Do I understand the type of lien, if any?

Final Step
-Have I asked for an explanation of terms I don't understand?
-Do I fully comprehend my financial obligations?

A fee agreement is a *contract* that identifies the respective responsibilities of the attorney and the client. A retainer is an advance *payment* made by the client to the attorney for future legal services, and its terms should be clearly explained within the fee agreement. Because fee agreements and retainers can be somewhat confusing due to terminology and formats, the following section provides an overview of these arrangements.

FEE AGREEMENTS

A fee agreement is also known as a retention letter, retainer agreement, engagement letter, legal services agreement, or letter of representation. It is a contract between you and your attorney that outlines the scope of your attorney's representation, the type of advance required, and your obligation to pay for legal services.

But this is not an ordinary contract.[2] An attorney owes a fiduciary duty to act in the client's best interests, and that duty governs every aspect of the attorney-client relationship.

Given an attorney's fiduciary obligations, it is surprising that the American Bar Association (ABA), which establishes ethical guidelines for lawyers, only requires written fee agreements for contingency and shared fee cases. The ABA recommends that fee agreements be "preferably in writing," but it is not a mandatory requirement for other matters. The ABA leaves it up to individual states to decide whether a written fee agreement is required for divorce, probate, criminal, or non-contingent civil cases. Additionally, while the ABA's Rules of Professional Conduct prohibit attorneys from making agreements that include unreasonable fees, a single, precise definition of "unreasonable fees" is not provided.

Let's review that again. The ABA prohibits unreasonable fees in a fee agreement but the term "unreasonable" is so vaguely defined that it can be difficult for non-lawyers to interpret. All 50 states, in some form, have adopted the ABA's rule regarding *unreasonable fees,* but without a clear definition. The ABA does not require a *written* fee agreement for all types of cases, even though attorneys as fiduciaries are obligated to act in their client's best interests. In some states, written fee agreements are required by state bar rules and state law, but in other states, written agreements are just recommended, except for contingency and shared fee cases.

As a result of ambiguous definitions for "unreasonable fees" and fee agreement requirements that vary by case type and state, clients are often left with limited guidance for interpreting legal terms and financial responsibilities. To address these concerns, the issue of unreasonable fees will be discussed at length in Chapter 7 and the following information provides more insight into fee agreements.

If your state only suggests a written fee agreement, ask your prospective attorney why they do not offer one. Their answer can help you decide if their arrangement is right for you. There may be other attorneys nearby who do provide written agreements, even when it is not required.

A written fee agreement is intended to protect the interests of both the client and the attorney by clearly outlining each party's responsibilities. The mystery about whether a fee agreement is required in your state makes it important to research the issue because a written contract helps reduce the potential for fee disputes. With a written fee agreement, you can hold the attorney accountable for their services if they do not perform as agreed, while the attorney can rely on your obligation to pay if they fulfill their duties.

The basic fee agreements for attorney services are hourly, flat fee, and contingency. A fourth arrangement, known as a "true retainer," is a specialized contract in which a client secures a lawyer's availability. Attorneys may also offer hybrid options. One example is a limited-scope representation or "unbundling" that limits the services the attorney will provide, and alternative fee arrangements (AFAs) that combine different billing methods to meet a client's needs. All of these agreements are discussed in this chapter. Because hourly billing is still the most common fee structure in many areas of law, the next three chapters examine hourly billing in greater detail.

Hourly Fee Agreement

This contract is based on hourly billing and permits an attorney and their legal staff to bill you for every minute they work on your case. As a result, clear descriptions of the legal work performed and the time spent on each task allow a client to make an informed review of the fees. The agreement typically identifies the attorney's hourly rate and, ideally, the hourly rates for their legal staff. The amount of retainer or advance payment should be clearly stated. Review the quoted hourly rates carefully and consider whether they are appropriate given the complexity of your case. A Federal Court has noted: "Nor do we approve the wasteful use of highly skilled and highly priced talent for matters easily delegable to non-professionals or less experienced associates."[3]

Flat Fee Agreement

A flat fee agreement, also known as a fixed fee agreement, is a contract with an attorney to provide a specific legal service for a one-time payment, regardless of the time and effort expended. The attorney should clearly outline the work that will be completed. The agreement can encompass an entire case or a selected service. Common examples are representing a client in an uncontested divorce for a fixed fee or agreeing to complete a trademark application for a one time charge. Flat fee agreements might also be used for a single traffic court appearance or the preparation and filing of a simple bankruptcy petition.

Contingency Fee Agreement

"Often contingent fee agreements are the only means possible for litigants to receive legal services ... contingent fees are still the poor man's key to the courthouse door. The contingent fee system allows persons who could not otherwise afford to assert their claims to have their day in court."[4]

In a contingency fee contract, you are not required to pay for legal services in advance. The attorney fees for your case will be based on a percentage of the recovery, but only if there is a settlement or judgment in your favor. The percentage charged by the attorney varies and will depend upon the type of case, the level of risk involved, and the probability of success. There may be litigation *costs* that you have to pay directly, or the attorney may cover these costs with the expectation of reimbursement when the case is resolved. Such costs include, but are not limited to, expert witness fees, process server costs, court costs, and filing fees. From the outset of your representation, you should be informed about who will be responsible for paying these expenses.

Contingency fee agreements are common in personal injury cases, but the American Bar Association expressly prohibits their use in divorce and criminal cases. Contingency agreements must be in writing, while written requirements for other fee agreements vary by jurisdiction.

True Retainer Agreement

A true retainer agreement is easily the most misunderstood type of contract. Under the terms of this agreement, an attorney's availability is secured for a particular period of time or for specific matters, regardless of whether any legal services are actually performed. It's essentially a payment, earned on receipt, for the lawyer's commitment to be available by declining other cases or potential clients that would interfere with their representation of a select client's legal issues.

Alternative Fee Arrangement (AFA)

This type of fee agreement evolved partly due to dissatisfaction with the hourly billing system. There are numerous types of AFAs, including capped fees, blended rates, fees per day, valuation pricing, and any billing variation that might work for both the attorney and client. The key point with this kind of agreement is to be certain that you understand exactly what legal services you will receive and the costs you will be required to pay.

Unbundling Legal Services

The ABA allows attorneys to unbundle their services by handling specific legal tasks without representing a client throughout the entire case. Unlike a flat-fee arrangement, which refers to a method of billing, unbundling refers to the limited scope of the attorney's representation. An unbundled service may be billed either hourly or on a flat or fixed fee basis. For example, you might complete the preliminary paperwork for a divorce on your own, while your attorney is retained only to negotiate and finalize a settlement.

Requirements governing unbundled legal services vary from state to state. Information about your state's rules regarding these services is available online through the American Bar Association's website.[5]

Once you receive the fee agreement, review it carefully. Some legal terms might not be clear. If you are not sure what something means or how it affects you, ask your attorney to explain. Examples of terms that may require further input are noted below.

FEE AGREEMENT TERMS TO REVIEW

Arbitration

Arbitration is certainly a valid option to resolve differences with your attorney, but it should be a choice, not a requirement. Note that there is a substantial difference between binding and non-binding arbitration. (see Chapter 8) Pay close attention to any clause in your fee agreement that states both parties agree to use binding arbitration for *all* disputes. If you encounter an arbitration clause in your fee agreement, ask your attorney to clarify the consequences. Arbitration can be an appropriate option for certain matters. However, depending upon the terms of your agreement, binding arbitration may waive your right to sue your attorney in a court of law for legal malpractice.

Charges for Billing Questions

Typically, clients are not billed for inquiring about charges on their invoices, because billing questions are usually considered administrative tasks. However, I reviewed a fee agreement that indicated the client might be obligated to pay for the attorney's time spent on defending disputed charges if they were found to be correct. Provisions like these illustrate the importance of reviewing a fee agreement before signing.

Deadline to Review Invoice for Errors

Your fee agreement may include a clause specifying that, if you fail to dispute charges on the invoice within a certain period, the fees will be considered valid. As a result, if you do not challenge any fees on the invoice promptly, your attorney may argue that you agreed to the charges. Their defensive use of this provision could affect your subsequent claims of excessive billing. Although the validity of the clause may be called into question, the potentially serious consequences give you another reason to review your invoices promptly.

Expenses

Your fee agreement should list the types of expenses you may incur during your litigation. While it is, of course, not possible to predict every potential expense, it is helpful to understand the costs you may be obligated to pay, such as filing fees, travel time, expert witness fees, transcription costs, court reporter fees, subpoena charges, postage and copying costs.

Liens

While liens are permitted as collection tools in many jurisdictions, their use is governed by professional conduct rules.[6] There are two primary types of liens: a **charging lien**, which attaches to any future recovery obtained through the attorney's efforts, and a **retaining lien**, which allows an attorney to retain your property or documents to secure unpaid fees. The availability and use of these liens vary by state. If your fee agreement references a lien, ask your attorney how it may affect you.

Minimum Increments

An agreement should clearly state if minimum billing increments apply. Attorneys and their staff may bill in increments for their time and charge for a minimum period, regardless of how long it took to perform a task. Minimum increments may be 0.1, 0.2, 0.25, or even 0.5 hours. For example, if the fee agreement sets a minimum rate of 0.2 per hour, you may be billed for 12 minutes of their time, even if a phone call only lasts 4 minutes. With hourly rates for attorneys reaching $500 an hour and more, the minutes add up. Increments of 0.1 of an hour are widely accepted, but anything greater should be questioned.

These terms, along with others, may be included in your agreement. If you do not fully understand any of the conditions in your agreement, ask your attorney for clarification. The terms of a fee agreement can have significant practical and financial consequences. Know precisely what you are signing.

RETAINERS

Golden Rule No. 1: A written fee agreement should clearly define the type of retainer required.[7]

A retainer is an advance payment for future legal services. How it is applied, whether it is refundable, when it can be used to pay legal fees, and at what point it becomes the attorney's property are governed by various state laws and the rules of the state bar association. The amount and type of retainer should be clearly stated in your fee agreement.

Because each state uses different terminology, it can be helpful to review the types of retainers permitted in your state to understand what is required for your case. Chapter 10 lists state bar websites and phone numbers for reference.

Important Note: Recently, the ABA discussed the ambiguity of the word "retainer" as it applies to fee agreements. According to the ABA, there is only one "true retainer," and all other fees paid in anticipation of receiving legal services should be labeled as advances.[8] Since the word "retainer" has several different definitions, this term can only add to the problems in disputing unreasonable fees.

For clarity, we'll use the term "retainer" as it is commonly understood, and it will be used interchangeably with "advance" to refer to a payment made in anticipation of legal services. The term "true retainer" will be used only when it applies to fees paid solely to secure the continuous availability of legal services for a defined period of time.

TYPES OF RETAINERS

Deposit

The most common retainer is a deposit to pay future legal fees as part of an hourly fee agreement. Since it is only a deposit, additional funds may be required once the original payment is exhausted. If the legal work is less than anticipated, you are entitled to a refund of any remaining funds after all fees and costs have been paid. An attorney may require a retainer as advance payment before they take your case to ensure that you will pay for their work, at least in the short run. This practice guards against an all-too-common scenario: clients who lose their case may become angry and refuse to pay, regardless of the quality of the legal services provided.

Your deposit is placed into a trust account, and as the attorney performs legal services, earned funds will be withdrawn from the trust account as outlined in the fee agreement until the retainer is depleted. Ideally, you should receive an invoice on a regular basis that clearly describes the work performed, the time spent on each task, the hourly billing rate, any expenses, and total charges for the designated time period.

When choosing legal representation, you might consider hiring the lawyer who asks for the lowest retainer. However, some lawyers use a small retainer as a marketing tool. Clients often discover that this initial retainer is wiped out within the first month. Suddenly, the client faces unexpected charges they did not anticipate.

Misunderstandings may occur if the agreement does not adequately explain how retainer funds will be used and when additional payments may be needed. Attorneys cannot predict the exact amount of legal fees that may be necessary, but explaining their billing practices can prevent future disputes. The fee agreement should state the policies for payment after the initial retainer is depleted. You may be required to replenish the retainer, pay the entire invoice balance when received or a payment schedule might be set up for your particular situation.

Engagement Fee

An engagement fee is a retainer that compensates the attorney for reserving their availability in advance and potentially declining other cases. You may find language in your fee agreement stating that this type of retainer is earned upon receipt and is nonrefundable. If you see this term in your agreement, ask your attorney about it. In one state, an attorney charged their client for an engagement fee without providing evidence that they had to decline other work. Upon review, the state's Supreme Court[9] found the attorney's engagement fee to be an unreasonable flat fee.

Flat Fee

A flat fee is the one-time retainer paid to an attorney for a specific legal service that is outlined in a flat-fee agreement. For instance, an attorney may charge $2,500 to draft a will, payable in advance, with the mutual understanding that is the total cost for preparing the document. Or you might make a payment of $15,000 to a criminal defense attorney to handle all pretrial proceedings. In each case, the single payment covers all of the attorney's work for that particular service.

One drawback of flat-fee retainers is that clients may not receive a breakdown of all the specific legal tasks to be performed. For example, a client agreed to a flat fee based on verbal descriptions and paid a significant advance. Subsequently, the client believed that several important and promised legal tasks were not performed. Because all the promised services were not clearly outlined in the flat fee agreement, it was difficult to assess whether the retainer was excessive and the relationship ended in a contested dispute.

When signing a flat-fee agreement, make certain that all conditions and promises are formalized in writing. Without clear terms, you risk paying a substantial sum upfront without meaningful accountability for the promised work. This was a lesson I learned personally, and one of the reasons for writing this book.

Nonrefundable Retainer

As the term implies, you would not be entitled to a refund if your representation ended prematurely. Some states have an outright ban on non-refundable retainers. Other states permit them, but only under specific circumstances. Some states have no ethical rule regarding non-refundable retainers.

So, once again, you will need to know if they are allowed in your state, and who better to ask than the attorney requesting it? In some cases, nonrefundable retainers have been the subject of fee disputes and ethical complaints, particularly when the terms are not clearly explained. Regardless of the nonrefundable label, attorneys are obligated to adhere to ethical standards and ensure their fees are reasonable.

The most important point to remember before signing a fee agreement is to make sure you are totally familiar with all of the terms. If anything is unclear, don't hesitate to request an explanation. Asking questions sets the tone for a transparent, professional relationship.

Understanding your fee agreement is an important step in protecting yourself from unreasonable fees and maintaining control over your legal costs.

---

1. American Bar Association, "Rule 1.5: Fees," in Model Rules of Professional Conduct, 2020.

2. *Balducci v. Cige*, 240 N.J. 574,592 (N.J. 2020).

3. *Ursic v. Bethlehem Mines*, 719 F.2d 670 (3d Cir. 1983).

4. *Silver Creek Invs., Inc. v. Whitten Const. Mgmt., Inc.*, 2013 OK CIV APP 49, ¶ 25, 307 P.3d 360, 369.

5. American Bar Association Unbundling Resource Center.

6. American Bar Association, "Rule 1.8 art. i: Current Clients: Specific Rules," in Model Rules of Professional Conduct, 2020.

7. *Dowling v. Chicago Options Associates, Inc.*, 875 NE 2d 1012 - Ill: Supreme Court 2007.

8. American Bar Association, Standing Committee on Ethics and Professional Responsibility, *Formal Opinion 505*, May 3, 2023.

9. *Attorney Grievance Commission v. Gregory Wayne Jones*, AG No.: 1, September Term 2021.

CHAPTER 4

ATTORNEY'S FEES

Legal bills go thru the roof, Hours billed without proof, I'll be in the poor house soon, but my lawyer sings a happy tune.

Intentional overbilling is more common than many people realize – estimates of fraudulent billing can range from 21% to over 33%, depending on the research methodology.[1] In this chapter, you'll learn about 18 common bill-padding practices that can unjustifiably increase legal fees. The following sections identify questionable billing practices and explain, with supporting analysis, why certain disputed charges may be considered unreasonable. Comparing your invoices to these examples will help you identify potentially unethical billing patterns and better evaluate whether the fees you are being charged accurately reflect the legal work performed.

POTENTIAL BILL-PADDING PRACTICES

1. **A lack of detail in describing an attorney's charges**
2. **A lack of detail in describing staff charges**
3. **Billing expenses above cost**
4. **Billing for tasks not performed**
5. **Block billing**
6. **Charges for clerical tasks billed by a paralegal**
7. **Charges for paralegal tasks billed by an attorney**
8. **Charges related to billing questions**
9. **Chipping**
10. **Churning**
11. **Duplicate billing**
12. **Excessive entries for document review**
13. **Excessive legal research**
14. **Excessive time to complete a task**
15. **Fees not in compliance with the fee agreement**
16. **High minimum increments**
17. **The overuse of "rounded" time estimates**
18. **Vague descriptions**

The following examples illustrate unreasonable legal fees that were successfully challenged. Certain details have been modified, and the timekeeper billing initials are fictional.

1. A lack of detail in describing an attorney's charges.

When an attorney bills by the hour, the invoice should include a description of the legal tasks performed on your behalf, the time it took to perform those tasks, and the hourly rate charged. However, if a task has only a simplistic description, such as a phone call, email, or a meeting, without additional clarifying information, the lack of specificity is unacceptable. For example, an entry on your invoice might look like this:

Date		Services	Hours	Rate	Amount
01/14/25	AB	Conference w/paralegal	.5	$450	$225.00

A descriptive billing record is essential for a client to determine the legitimacy of fees. Yet, attorney AB does not provide the subject matter or the purpose of the conference. Without that information, it would be difficult to evaluate the legitimacy of the fee. Shouldn't you have the right to know the purpose of the $225 charge?

Courts have found that you do have that right because imprecise or incomplete entries are unacceptable. One court stated, "*Time entries for telephone calls, conferences, and letters must state the purpose or nature of the service and the persons involved.*"[2] If you find this type of entry on your invoice, you have a valid basis for a dispute.

An attorney is ethically obligated to charge reasonable fees and the fees should reflect the actual legal tasks performed. As one court explained, "*Reasonable attorney fees must be based upon actual services performed by the attorney and upon the value of those services.*"[3] In this example, because the legal services performed during the conference could not be identified, their value could not be determined and were successfully challenged.

2. A lack of detail in describing staff charges

The same rule of adequate descriptions applies to an attorney's staff. They should provide specific information when explaining their charges. A law clerk or paralegal should describe the tasks performed so you can assess the reasonableness of the fee.

Date		Services	Hours	Rate	Amount
02/10/25	CD	File Administration	1	$200	$200.00

Paralegal CD billed a client $200 for "file administration." This vague description is highly questionable because it does not provide enough information for the client to determine whether it is substantive legal work that could be appropriately billed by a paralegal. A federal court expressed a similar concern, stating, "*Nothing about 'file administration' suggests legal work.*"[4] When analyzing the charges claimed by your attorney's staff, note that they should also provide the same level of detail as the attorney. If they do not, you have the right to question those charges.

3. Billing expenses above cost

Charges for legal expenses (e.g., transcripts, messenger services, copies, or filing fees) should reflect the lawyer's actual cost for the services provided.

Date		Expenses			Amount
03/11/25		**Copy Charges 680 pages**			**$204**

In this example, an attorney billed a client 30 cents per page for copying a large volume of documents. Several issues arise with this charge. First, the client's fee agreement did not specify the cost per copy. Second, the description of copying costs was too vague to substantiate the expense. As courts have held that attorneys may recover copy and postage costs with proper notice, the fee agreement should clearly specify potential expenses.

If the attorney wants to add a premium to these claimed expenses, they must first obtain permission through disclosure in the fee agreement. Before signing, carefully read the fee agreement to identify and agree to the potential expenses that may occur during the representation. The American Bar Association (ABA), the organization that sets the ethical standards for the legal profession, states, *"[I]t is impermissible for a lawyer to create an additional source of profit for the law firm beyond that which is contained in the provision of professional services themselves."*[5]

If black-and-white copies cost less than 15 cents per page, you can question why an attorney charged an additional 15 cents per page. An attorney who adds a surcharge can be challenged and required to explain potentially "unreasonable" expenses. Courts have stated that an attorney should produce *"evidence showing the nature of the documents copied, including how they were used or intended to be used in the case."* [6]

4. Billing for tasks not performed.

Look over your invoice closely, as charges may appear for legal work that was not performed. During arbitration, a client disputed a $1,400 fee because he had not received a copy of a motion allegedly drafted by the attorney. When the client questioned the fee, Attorney EF was unable to provide the document, and the charge was deducted without further discussion. Additionally, this description is vague and warrants a challenge because it is unclear what motion was filed. Another question to ask is why a clerical task (filing) was billed at an attorney's rate.

Date		Services	Hours	Rate	Amount
04/02/25	EF	Draft and file motion	3.5	$400	$1,400

Despite an attorney's ethical duty to charge a reasonable fee for legal services, intentional overbilling can still occur. For example, a bankruptcy attorney was found to have filed a *"claim for expenses never incurred and for legal work not performed."*[7] Another attorney was sanctioned *"for manipulating his billing records for the sole purpose of achieving a bonus."*[8] Additionally, in yet another instance, an attorney accepted a retainer and *"failed to perform any work on the matter or to take any action to preserve any claims the client may have had."*[9] Although these cases represent only a sample, the fact remains that overbilling does occur despite ethical guidelines.

In an extreme example, an attorney charged for *"trial preparation"* when he was on vacation in Europe and billed *"hundreds of fictitious hours of legal work."*[10] The actions of the attorney led the Court to state, *"It is the Court's hope that all attorneys who read this opinion will be reminded that the practice of law is a public trust to be sacredly guarded and not a right given to any person."* Monitor your invoice carefully so you can avoid paying for legal tasks not performed.

5. Block billing

Block billing is the practice of lumping several different legal tasks together into a single charge.

Date		Services	Hours	Rate	Amount
04/10/25	GH	Meeting w/client and paralegal; TC to OC; Research Motion; Draft Documents; Email to cl	4	$450	$1,800

The specific amount of time for each legal activity is not identified separately. This questionable billing practice is easy to recognize and, unfortunately, a relatively common occurrence. When Attorney GH combines multiple legal services into a single charge, it becomes nearly impossible for the client to determine the reasonableness of each task.

Without information on the length of phone calls or the types of documents prepared, a client cannot assess the validity of the billing entries. A federal court addressed the questionable practice of block billing, stating that the practice of "*lumping*" tasks together *"prevents an accurate determination of the reasonableness of the time expended in a case."*[11]

Another court noted that the practice of block billing impedes the court's ability to assess the reasonable amount of time on each task,[12] *"The party seeking fees bears the burden of proving that the hours claimed were reasonably expended on the litigation, and he can meet that burden only by presenting evidence that is adequate for the court to determine what hours should be included in the reimbursement."*

This practice is so widespread that an attorney in a continuing education course actually recommended that attorneys avoid recording time in even increments and suggested entering times like 0.90, 1.10, or 1.20 to prevent the *appearance* of block billing. Once you identify block billing on your invoice, it's time to discuss this billing practice with your attorney and request that they provide additional information so you can review the reasonableness of each charge.

6. Charges for clerical tasks billed by a paralegal.

With the appropriate experience and education, a paralegal is a valuable asset to clients and attorneys. A paralegal can save the client money and allow the attorney to better utilize their time by providing legal services at a lower rate. That said, the paralegal's billed tasks must involve substantive legal work that uses their training. Examples of substantive legal work include conducting legal research and drafting documents under an attorney's supervision, as opposed to clerical work, which involves administrative tasks such as filing and copying documents. It is unacceptable to use a paralegal to perform clerical tasks and charge the paralegal's rate.

Date		Services	Hours	Rate	Amount
05/10/25	IJ	Copy client emails	.2	$200	$40
05/11/25	IJ	Copy docs for Attorney	.3	$200	$60

This example illustrates Paralegal IJ charging the client $200 an hour for copying emails and documents. Clerical tasks, like those mentioned above, are typically considered overhead expenses by the courts and should not be billed separately.

The U.S. Supreme Court stated that *"purely clerical or secretarial tasks should not be billed at a paralegal rate regardless of who performs them."*[13]

When you receive your invoice, review the entries very carefully. Examine the tasks performed by a paralegal and question whether they are appropriate. Discuss with your attorney the possibility of secretarial or clerical charges being billed at a paralegal's rate.

If you find ambiguous entries, request a more transparent description of the services performed. Issues related to paralegal billings are common and can lead to significant overcharges. The next chapter explores this problem in greater detail, providing examples of clients who were overbilled because of improper invoicing.

7. Charges for clerical/paralegal tasks performed by an attorney.

In this case, Attorney KL charged their hourly rate of $350 for creating a file. Not only was the description of the task vague, but it should also have been performed by clerical staff.

Date		Services	Hours	Rate	Amount
06/10/25	KL	File Creation	1	$350	$350.00

"It is well settled that costs associated with clerical tasks are typically considered overhead expenses reflected in an attorney's hourly billing rate and are not properly reimbursable."[14]

What are clerical tasks? Several courts answer that question by stating that filing and document organization are clerical and should be included in the firm's overhead. Although this is not a definitive answer for all cases, similar tasks should be questioned if they appear on your invoice. When you identify a clerical task, ask your attorney for clarification, and it then becomes the attorney's responsibility to explain why they charge an attorney's rate for clerical work.[15]

Date		Services	Hours	Rate	Amount
06/10/25	KL	Calendar hearing dates for motion & response	.2	$350	$70.00

Attorney KL also billed the client for routine calendaring, a task that a paralegal or a clerk could handle and should not be charged at an attorney's rate.

A court of appeals found that "*legal service rates are not applicable when an attorney provides services that could have been easily delegated to a non-professional.*"[16]

When reviewing your invoice, identify tasks billed by the attorney that could have been handled by a paralegal. Of course, distinguishing a paralegal task from one that requires an attorney's expertise can be difficult, but there is a simple solution: ask your attorney! Question why you were charged an attorney's rate for filing a document or calendaring a motion.

For additional guidance, Chapter 5 provides a list of tasks that courts have considered clerical or paralegal in nature and identifies legal services that courts have determined are not appropriately billed at attorney rates. If you notice questionable charges, challenge the fee and request an explanation.

8. Charges related to billing

A lawyer should not charge for administrative tasks unless specifically outlined in the fee agreement.[17] Questions about billing or account statements are generally considered administrative tasks and should not be billed as legal services. If you notice this type of fee on your invoice, bring it to your attorney's attention for clarification.

Date		Services	Hours	Rate	Amount
07/10/25	MN	Call client re: billing issues	.2	$150	$30.00

In this instance, paralegal MN returned the client's call regarding a billing issue and billed for their time. A law review article discussing best billing practices noted that discussions about legal bills, invoicing, and related activities should not be billed separately as they "*should be viewed as overhead costs for the firm.*"[18] The article cited numerous supporting court decisions regarding improper charges for time spent on the administration of fee issues.

If you identify charges for billing questions on your invoice, it's time to bring the charges to your attorney's attention.

9. Chipping

This tactic exemplifies how creative lawyers can be, as chipping could be considered the opposite of block billing. Chipping is breaking down one task into several smaller tasks, resulting in more time expended and, thus, a more significant fee.

In one disciplinary case, an attorney was suspended from the practice of law because the Court found she *"failed to ensure that her charges were reasonable."* [19] Among the stipulated violations, the Court provided examples of the attorney billing .25 of an hour to review a document and another .25 of an hour to sign the same document. The attorney also routinely billed .25 of an hour to simply sign documents such as stipulated orders and pleadings. When reviewing legal bills, if you notice a series of small charges that seem unnecessary or excessive, ask your attorney to explain why related fees were divided into separate increments.

Date		Services	Hours	Rate	Amount
08/10/25	MN	Review msg from client	.2	$150	$30
08/12/25	MN	Rec'd email from client	.2	$150	$30
08/12/25	MN	Scan email to file	.2	$150	$30
08/13/25	MN	Conf w/Atty re: email	.2	$150	$30

In this example, an invoice shows that a client contacted the attorney's paralegal, MN, and left a brief message about a check mailed to the attorney.

When the paralegal didn't respond, the client sent a follow-up email. The paralegal then made a copy of the email and asked the attorney what to do about the check. Although the underlying task was simple, it generated a larger fee because each step was billed separately at the minimum increment. A state's arbitration committee noted: *"[B]illing every task separately may artificially inflate time entries."*[20]

10. Churning

Churning is the practice of creating excessive and unnecessary tasks to inflate a client's fees. If you suspect this is happening in your case, contact your attorney and ask for an explanation.

Date		Services	Hours	Rate	Amount
09/10/25	QR	Sent ltr to OC re: Car	.2	$150	$30
09/10/25	QR	Email to OC re: Car	.2	$150	$30
09/10/25	QR	Sent facx to OC re: Car	.2	$150	$30
09/11/25	QR	Sent ltr to OC re: Car	.2	$150	$30

During my time practicing law, I observed numerous instances in which this particular billing practice became a point of dispute.

In one particular case, the opposing counsel's office sent faxes, emails, letters, and phone messages almost daily, instead of consolidating the information into a single document. This approach, often carried out by multiple paralegals, resulted in duplicative work and generated unnecessary fees.

The above entries resulted from a non-emergency situation in which a community property vehicle was to be transferred to the opposing party at a future date. A simple letter could have resolved the issue. Instead, redundant paperwork was prepared with no apparent purpose other than to increase the client's bill.

A law professor discussed a fairly common tactic used by law firms in a big city. *"These firms generate business by taking on new clients in divorce cases and churning the file until the client runs out of money for legal fees. Then the firm withdraws."*[21]

A federal court explained why this type of fee is improper: *"To state the obvious, it is not reasonable for an attorney to charge for time spent on tasks that lack any reasonable prospect of creating value for the client. After all, to charge for that time would benefit only the attorney, not the client. Yet the practice is sufficiently widespread that a term has been coined for it: churning."*[22]

11. Duplicate billing

When an identical charge appears on your invoice several times, it could be an example of duplicate billing. The charge might be an error, but it occurs often enough on invoices to recognize it as a potential issue. There are several ways that duplicate billing can appear on your invoice.

For example, an attorney and a paralegal may both inadvertently charge for performing the same task, or a vague description may be listed on two different dates, with the same amount charged each time.

When checking for this error, check the date and make sure the amount, and subject matter are identical. If so, highlight it as an issue to discuss with your attorney.

Date		Services	Hours	Rate	Amount
10/06/25	ST	**Receive and Review Order**	.2	$400	$80
10/06/25	UV	**Review Order**	.2	$180	$36

In this example, paralegal UV billed for reviewing filings that attorney ST had already received and reviewed. The attorney read the documents and correctly billed for his time. However, the paralegal failed to provide sufficient details about the necessity of reviewing the same document a second time, so it is impossible to determine if the charge was appropriate.

The U.S. Supreme Court stated that an attorney *"should make a good-faith effort to exclude from a fee request hours that are excessive, redundant, or otherwise unnecessary."*[23]

12. Excessive entries for document review

For a document review fee to be reasonable, it must be utilized to produce a response or perform a specified task. A fee is unreasonable when an attorney bills for *"simply reading the work product of another lawyer."*[24]

Date		Services	Hours	Rate	Amount
11/03/25	WX	Draft Responsive Brief	8	$400	$3,200
11/03/25	YZ	Review Brief	1	$350	$350
11/04/25	AB	Review Brief	1	$350	$350

Attorney WX drafted a document that was appropriately billed, but it was reviewed by two other attorneys, YZ and AB. Neither attorney provided an explanation for the necessity of reviewing the original document. Their fees were questioned and subsequently reduced because the attorneys could not justify the excessive review.

13. Excessive legal research

It is the lawyer's responsibility to explain the legal research conducted on your behalf.

Date		Services	Hours	Rate	Amount
03/01/25	GH	Research appellate brief	8	$170	$1,360
03/02/25	GH	Research appellate brief	6	$170	$1,020
03/03/25	GH	Research appellate brief	7	$170	$1,190

In this example, law clerk GH provided extensive research on a topic but failed to provide sufficient information that adequately described the work performed. The Court significantly reduced the fees because of "*numerous instances of documentation and specification that do not adequately describe the legal work for which the client is being billed. This makes it impossible for the court to verify the reasonableness of the billings, either as to the necessity of the particular service or the amount of time expended on a given legal task.*"[25]

14. Excessive time to complete a task.

Unsubstantiated charges for large blocks of time are easy to identify, but can be difficult to dispute. As you carefully review each entry on your attorney's invoice, you may see time entries with a questionable number of hours for a single task without an adequate description of the work performed on your behalf.

Date		Services	Hours	Rate	Amount
12/10/25	CD	Prepare for Trial	5	$400	$2,000
12/11/25	CD	Prepare for Trial	4	$400	$1,600
12/12/25	CD	Prepare for Trial	6	$400	$2,400
12/13/25	CD	Prepare for Trial	8	$400	$3,200

Attorney CD billed substantial blocks of time for pre-trial preparation but failed to provide even a basic explanation of what the work described as "prepare for trial" entailed. The vague wording of these large time segments made it impossible for the client to evaluate the reasonableness of the fees charged.

A Federal Court of Appeal addressed this billing practice by reducing the requested fees due to vague and excessive entries. The court questioned counsel because *"many of the time entries submitted were so vague that there is no way to discern whether the hours billed were reasonable with no additional explanation regarding the subject or necessity of the review."*

Additionally, because of the specific circumstances in this case, the Court ruled it had the discretion *"to deny a fee request altogether when, under the circumstances, the amount requested is outrageously excessive."*[26]

Estimating how much time an attorney should spend on a given task is nearly impossible for most clients. Still, you are entitled to enough information to understand what you are being charged for—especially when an invoice lists a significant number of hours accompanied by only a vague description.

15. Fees not in compliance with the terms of the fee agreement.

Your fee agreement is a contract, and your attorney is obligated to comply with its terms. If you monitor the costs and expenses associated with your legal representation, you can avoid unexpected charges and potential disputes.

Date		Services	Hours	Rate	Amount
05/10/25	DE	Telephone conference with client on 5/8	1	$500	$500.00

In this case, attorney DE accurately described a conference with the client. While the client acknowledged that the length of the phone call was accurate, the attorney's rate differed from what was stated in the fee agreement. The fee agreement clearly indicated that the attorney charged $400 an hour. The attorney did not provide the client with any notice that his rate was going to increase. The charge was corrected when brought to the attorney's attention.

When reviewing your invoice, compare the hourly rates charged to those specified in your fee agreement. If you find a discrepancy, notify your attorney and point out the issue.

Your attorney is obligated to notify you of any hourly rate increases in advance. This information should be spelled out in your fee agreement.

The American Bar Association states that an attorney shall provide notice of changes in the attorney's rate structure: "*Any changes in the basis or rate of the fee or expenses shall also be communicated to the client.*"[27]

16. High minimum increments

Your fee agreement may include language that allows the attorneys and their staff to charge clients in high minimum time increments, such as .25 of an hour (15 minutes). As a result, attorneys and staff members are permitted to charge you for both actual time worked and any "unused" time up to the minimum.

Date		Services	Hours	Rate	Amount
06/10/25	KL	Telephone call to client re: meeting with Atty	.25	$180	$45.00

Paralegal KL called and informed the client that the attorney wanted to meet the next day at 10:00 a.m. Although the call lasted less than two minutes, the paralegal charged 0.25 of an hour, or 15 minutes, for the call. The problem? The paralegal billed an extra thirteen minutes but performed no discernible work during that time, due to the office policy of billing in 0.25-of-an-hour increments.

Although you may have already agreed to high increments in your fee agreement, question this practice if you notice short calls and tasks that seem to take less time than the stated minimum. Excessive use of high minimum increments can lead to substantial and unreasonable fees because you may be charged a fee when no actual work is performed on your behalf. While a 0.1 of an hour minimum increment is generally accepted by the courts, rates of .25 of an hour and greater have come under scrutiny.

A federal court discussed the argument against quarter-hour intervals: *"[B]illing in quarter-hour increments [is] unreasonable since many tasks [telephone calls and reviewing documents] simply do not take that long."*[28] The court felt a fee request did not have the *"extensive, detailed support"* that would show *"each billing record was an accurate representation of the time spent on the case."*

17. Obvious Use of "Rounded" Time Estimates

Date		Services	Hours	Rate	Amount
04/10/25	CD	Meeting with client	5	$400	$2,000
04/10/25	CD	Research issue for brief	4	$400	$1,600
04/10/25	CD	Research issue for brief	6	$400	$2,400
04/10/25	CD	Research issue for brief	8	$400	$3,200
04/12/25	CD	Draft pleadings	8	$400	$3,200

An invoice contained charges that were all rounded to the nearest hour with vague task descriptions.

Attorney CD billed the client for legal services by rounding each task to the nearest hour. This practice is questionable, since it is doubtful that every task was completed in precise hourly increments, and it is a typical example of overbilling. A federal court reviewing similar billing practices found them entirely unacceptable, noting that such records do not "*provide the Court with sufficient evidence to determine the amount of time spent on particular tasks. Moreover, it results in a substantial windfall to Plaintiff's counsel.*"[29]

This example is not an isolated case. In a previously mentioned survey, 21% of the lawyers questioned overcharged their hourly clients by rounding up the number of hours worked.[30]

18. Vague Descriptions

Although vague billing descriptions have been discussed, this issue is so common that the following examples, explicitly identified by courts as problematic, deserve another look.

Ask yourself, "Can I determine from the description what work was performed and why it was necessary?" If the answer is no, flag the entry and ask for more information.

Conference
Email
Fact investigation
Hearing preparation
Prepare for conference

Prepare for discovery
Prepare for hearing
Research
Review documents
Review records
Voicemail
Work on brief

State and federal courts have found it difficult to determine whether the time allocated to these tasks was reasonable without further explanation of the vague descriptions.[31] One federal court reduced attorney fees because" *The contested entries for file review fail to indicate what is being reviewed or the purpose for the review and are properly excluded as inadequate and vague. For example, 'review e-mail' provides no information regarding the content or purpose of the email. Similarly, an entry that merely states, 'fact investigation' does not indicate the purpose or content of the investigation."*[32]

Chapter 9 provides a more extensive list of problematic vague descriptions.

A FINAL POINT

It can be disheartening to learn that some attorneys intentionally misrepresent the time spent on legal services to increase their fees. Even more disturbing is to discover questionable practices were recommended in a continuing education course for attorneys.

An online course on billing practices suggested that nearly everything an attorney does can be billed if the right wording is used.

The course material implied that lawyers could also be intentionally vague if it served their interests.

The course suggested that, in order to avoid a task being labeled as secretarial, work that is typically non-billable, the wording should convey a higher level of importance. Additionally, the course advised against billing in even time increments (e.g., 1 hour, 2 hours, etc.), not for the sake of accuracy, but to avoid the appearance of block billing.

In her article "*Lying to Clients,*" Professor Lerman interviewed 20 lawyers in a scholarly effort to address the issue of lawyers deceiving their clients. She states, "*Nearly all of the lawyers interviewed reported some amount of deception in practices relating to billing clients.*[33]

This chapter will help you recognize billing practices that may improperly inflate legal fees. By identifying questionable charges on your invoice, you will be better prepared to document and challenge unreasonable attorney fees.

---

1. H. Dennis Beaver, Esq., "Overbilled by Your Lawyer? You're Not Alone" *Kiplinger Newsletter,* January 9, 2024.
2. *In Re Johnson,* 317 B.R. 347 (Bankr. C.D. Ill. 2004).
3. *In re C.L.W.,* 2024-Ohio-1519, 2024 WL 1714504, ¶ 59 (12th Dist.).
4. *Marsh v. Digital Equipment Corp.,* 699 F. Supp. 1411 (D. Ariz. 1988).
5. American Bar Association Standing Committee on Ethics and Professional Responsibility, *Billing for Professional Fees, Disbursement Disbursements and Other Expenses,* Formal Opinion 93-379, 1993.

6. *Cobb v. City of Roswell, Ga,* 987 F. Supp. 2d 1319 (N.D. Ga. 2013).

7. *In re Campbell,* 140 BR 35 - Bankr. Court, ED New York 1992

8. *Disciplinary Proceedings Against Siderits,* 824 NW 2d 812 - Wis: Supreme Court 2013.

9. *Disciplinary Proceedings Against Gillette,* 895 NW 2d 1 - Wis: Supreme Court 2017.

10. *US v. Genova,* 167 F. Supp. 2d 1021 - Dist. Court, ND Illinois 2001167 F.Supp.2d 1021 (2001).

11. *Guidry v. Clare,* 442 F. Supp. 2d 282 (E.D. Va. 2006).

12. *Merrick v. Scott,* Dist. Court, ND (Texas 2011).

13. *Missouri v. Jenkins,* 491 U.S. 274 (1989).

14. *Brandt v. Astrue,* 2009 WL 1727472, at *4 (D. Or. June 16, 2009).

15. *Nadarajah v. Holder,* 569 F. 3d 906 (9th Cir. 2009); *Davis v. City & County of San Francisco,* 976 F.2d 1536, 1543 (9th Cir 1992) (citing *Missouri v. Jenkins,* 491 U.S. 274, (1989); see also *Keith v. Volpe,* 644 F.Supp. 1312, 1316 (C.D.Cal. 1986).

16. *Spegon v. Catholic Bishop of Chicago,* 175 F.3d 544 (7th Cir. 1999).

17. American Bar Association Standing Committee on Ethics and Professional Responsibility, *Billing for Professional Fees, Disbursement Disbursements and Other Expenses,* Formal Opinion 93-379, 1993.

18. Johnson, Laura et al., "Establishing Best Billing Practices Through Billing Guidelines: Fostering Trust and Transparency on Legal Costs," *University of Arkansas at Little Rock Law Review* 39, no. 1 (2016): 1–24.

19. *Board Of Professional Responsibility, Wyoming State v. Casper,* 318 P. 3d 790 - Wyo: Supreme Court 2014.

20. State Bar of California, "Analysis of Potential Bill Padding and Other Billing Issues", *Arbitration Advisory* 2016-02, 2016.

21. Simon, Roy (1994) "Gross Profts? An Introduction to a Program on Legal Fees," *Hofstra Law Review*: Vol. 22 : Iss. 3 , Article 2.

22. *Gurule v. Land Guardian, Inc.*, 912 F.3d 252 (5th Cir. 2018).

23. *Hensley v. Eckerhart,* 461 U.S. 424 (1983).

24. *Matter of Navis Realty, Inc.,* 126 B.R. 137 (Bankr. E.D.N.Y. 1991).

25. *Role Models America, Inc. v. Brownlee,* 353 F.3d 962 (D.C. Cir. 2004); *In re Olson,* 884 F.2d 1415, 1428 (D.C. Cir. 1989); *U. Slate, Tile Composition v. G M Roofing,* 732 F.2d 495, 502 n. 2 (6th Cir. 1984).

26. *Clemens v. N.Y. Cent. Mut. Fire Ins. Co.,* 903 F.3d 396 (3d Cir. 2018).

27. American Bar Association, "Rule 1.5: Fees," in *Model Rules of Professional Conduct,* 2020.

28. *Swisher v. U.S.,* 262 F. Supp. 2d 1203 (D. Kan. 2003).

29. *George v. GTE Directories Corp.,* 114 F. Supp. 2d 1281 (M.D. Fla. 2000).

30. Weiss, Debra Cassens, "Red-Flag Billing Practices Chronicled; Report Finds 'upbilling' by 21 Percent of Law Firms." *ABA Journal,* March 28, 2017.

31. *LV v. New York City Dept. of Educ.,* 700 F. Supp. 2d 510 (S.D.N.Y. 2010); *In Re Thomas* (Bankr. C.D. Ill 2024); *Fralick v. Plumbers & Pipefitters Nat'l Pension Fund,* 2011 WL 487754 (N.D. Tex. 2011).

32. *Tobin v. Gordon,* 614 F. Supp. 2d 514 - Dist. Court, D. (Delaware 2009).

33. Lerman, Lisa, "Lying to Clients," *University of Pennsylvania Law Review* 138 (1990): 659–760.

Chapter 5

Paralegals: Lawyer's Pot of Gold

Paralegals have an ethical obligation to bill responsibly. What can go wrong?

An educated and experienced paralegal is a cost-effective asset for clients and an efficient time-saver for attorneys. Paralegals offer excellent value for their hourly rate when they perform substantive legal work. Unfortunately, in some cases, paralegal billing practices have been used as profit centers that raise concerns about inflated legal fees. In this chapter, you'll learn how to distinguish between fair paralegal charges and fees that may cross ethical lines. Although paralegals are not required to be licensed in any state, you may still be billed hundreds of dollars per hour for their services. This chapter will help you evaluate whether those charges are justified, based on the type and quality of work performed in your case.

The American Bar Association's Model Guideline No. 1 for the utilization of paralegal services states:

"A lawyer is responsible for all of the professional actions of a paralegal performing services at the lawyer's direction and should take reasonable measures to ensure that the paralegal's conduct is consistent with the lawyer's obligations under the rules of professional conduct of the jurisdiction in which the lawyer practices."[1]

The National Federation of Paralegal Associations states, *"A paralegal shall ensure that all timekeeping and billing records prepared by the paralegal are thorough, accurate, honest, and complete."*[2]

The ABA and NFPA require fees to be accurate, honest, and in compliance with professional obligations, yet billing issues persist for a simple reason: a failure to properly monitor and manage questionable paralegal charges.

This is especially true when clients are often unaware that clerical tasks, such as copying documents, should not be billed at paralegal rates that may exceed $200 per hour.

The ABA defines a paralegal as *"[A] person qualified by education, training or work experience who is employed or retained by a lawyer, law office, corporation, governmental agency or other entity and who performs specifically delegated substantive legal work for which a lawyer is responsible."*[3]

The U.S. Supreme Court in *Missouri v. Jenkins*[4] clarifies this matter: *"Of course, purely clerical or secretarial tasks should not be billed at a paralegal rate, regardless of who performs them."* The Court went on to explain that the *"...services rendered by the paralegal must be legal in nature, i.e., 'factual investigation, locating and interviewing witnesses, assistance with depositions, interrogatories and document production, compilation of statistical and financial data, checking legal citations and drafting correspondence.'"*

Clerical and secretarial services should not appear on your invoice as billable hours unless specifically outlined in your fee agreement. Numerous state and federal cases[5] have held that a reasonable attorney would include their office overhead (i.e., secretarial and clerical services) in their hourly billing rate.

The following examples illustrate paralegal charges that have been identified as inconsistent with professional billing standards.

Date		Services	Hours	Rate	Amount
05/15/25	KL	Copy Client File	.5	$150	$75
05/15/25	KL	Print/Save Docs to File	.2	$150	$30
05/15/25	KL	Create Client File	1	$150	$150
05/15/02	KL	Prepare Cover Letter	.5	$150	$75
05/15/25	KL	Track Package	.2	$150	$30

When reviewing your invoice, look for clerical tasks such as copying, collating, scanning, or filing that may be incorrectly billed at higher rates. These tasks do not normally qualify as substantive legal work and should not be charged as such. If you find charges like these on your invoice, contact your attorney and ask why you were billed for clerical services. Be sure to keep a record of all communications with your attorney for future reference.

Of course, since we are dealing with attorneys, there will always be a counterargument. Two exceptions *might* allow clerical or secretarial work to be billed: first, if it is agreed upon in your fee agreement, and second, if the clerical services are essential to legal representation and are typically billed in the marketplace.[6] However, these scenarios are the exceptions rather than the rule. Once you challenge these fees, it will be up to the attorney to provide an adequate explanation.

WHAT IS THE DIFFERENCE BETWEEN CLERICAL AND PARALEGAL TASKS?

Understanding the distinction between clerical and secretarial services, and those properly performed by a paralegal, can be challenging. What exactly is the difference between non-legal and legal work? How do you determine the difference between clerical/secretarial staff performing tasks that should not be billed and paralegal tasks that should be compensated? The fact that numerous courts have weighed in on these questions demonstrates how some lawyers attempt to stretch the boundaries between ethical and unethical billing practices.

To help clarify the distinction, the following examples illustrate clerical and secretarial tasks that courts in various states have deemed non-compensable.

EXAMPLES OF NON-BILLABLE CLERICAL WORK

Alabama: Purely clerical tasks included indexing and binding of deposition exhibits, printing documents, converting documents to a PDF file, and developing a trial notebook including exhibits, because they are not "traditionally done by an attorney." Inclusion of these hours at a paralegal rate is unreasonable.[7]

Arizona: These purely clerical tasks are not compensable: filing, uploading, formatting, sequencing, Bates-stamping, proofreading (as opposed to substantive revision of) documents, calendaring dates, and organizing the case file.[8]

California: Billing for calendaring and scheduling, scanning, securing rental cars and other travel arrangements, reviewing invoices, and downloading PDF orders onto an iPad, among other things, are clerical tasks and non-compensable.[9]

Connecticut: "[C]lerical services such as making telephone calls, proofreading, and preparing documents are not compensable."[10]

Colorado: "Activities such as reviewing mail, making deposits and disbursements, and reconciling bank statements appear to be clerical in nature and, absent a more specific showing, should not be separately compensable." [11]

Indiana: Courts in the Seventh Circuit have identified a variety of administrative tasks, including organizing file folders, document preparation, copying or faxing documents, scheduling matters, and mailing letters.[12]

Kentucky: Receiving, reviewing, and processing files is clerical work because it "does not require substantive legal knowledge ."[13]

Louisiana: A Court agreed that entries for downloading and/or saving files, hardware setup and testing, filing pleadings, and calling the Court about filing pleadings are clerical tasks.[14]

New Jersey: Administrative tasks are not usually compensated and generally include, but are not limited to, opening a file in a database, entering case updates in a management system, mailing letters, copying documents, calendaring deadlines, confirming contact information, and communicating with a process server or court clerk.[15]

New York: A court reviewed the time sheets of an attorney who inappropriately billed his attorney rate for clerical tasks, such "as sending and receiving faxes, requesting and receiving medical records, serving papers, and hand-delivering courtesy copies of filings to the courthouse."[16]

Oklahoma: Charges "for time spent in copying documents and in doing other secretarial tasks, rather than substantive legal work" are not recoverable as paralegal/legal assistant fees.[17]

Oregon: Clerical or secretarial costs are part of an attorney's office overhead and are reflected in their billing rate.[18]

Texas: Time spent organizing the case file and entering data into a case management computer program is not billable legal work.[19]

Washington: "[C]ompensation for preparing pleadings for duplication, preparing and delivering copies, requesting copies, and obtaining and delivering a docket sheet" is not within the realm of "reasonable attorney fees."[20]

EXAMPLES OF PARALEGAL WORK THAT COURTS HAVE FOUND TO BE PROPERLY BILLABLE

"Substantive legal work" refers to legal tasks performed by a paralegal and properly billed to a client. State and federal courts have addressed the reasonableness of such billing practices.

Arkansas: "[W]ork done by paralegals is compensable if it is work that would have been done by an attorney."[21]

Colorado: Paralegal charges are viewed as "surrogate attorney fees" because an attorney would have performed the work if a paralegal had not been employed in their place.[22]

Delaware: A family law court defined substantive legal work and reiterated the Supreme Court's findings in *Missouri v. Jenkins:* "[T]he danger of charging off a secretary's services as those of a paralegal is very real and present, thereby mandating that certain information be provided by the supervising attorney before paralegal fees can be awarded by this Court in the future."

Those criteria are as follows: substantive legal work which may be performed by legal assistants and billed at the market rate includes but is not limited to, such activities as:

(a) Factual investigation, including locating and interviewing witnesses;
(b) Assistance with depositions, interrogatories, and document production;
(c) Compilation of statistical and financial data;
(d) Checking legal citations;
(e) Correspondence with clients, opposing counsel, courts
(f) Preparing/reviewing/answering petitions and other pleadings."[23]

District of Columbia: Drafting legal memoranda, drafting motions to dismiss, conducting legal research, and reading and responding to emails were consistent with the type of work appropriate for a paralegal.[24]

Florida: When awarding attorneys' fees, the court must consider the time and labor of paralegals "who contributed *non-clerical, meaningful legal support* to the matter involved."[25]

Illinois: "In determining whether a task is administrative in nature, the relevant inquiry is "whether the work was sufficiently complex to justify the efforts of a paralegal, as opposed to an employee at the next rung lower on the pay-scale ladder."[26]

Oklahoma: Compensation of paralegal fees is limited to work for services performed, which otherwise would have had to have been performed by an attorney at a higher rate.[27]

Texas: "Examples of tasks that the Court considers to be 'substantive legal work' are: contacting state agencies to request information, drafting deposition notices or trial subpoenas, and drafting most documents that will be filed with the Court."[28]

West Virginia: The court discussed examples of paralegal work as tasks normally performed by an attorney, and reiterated the US Supreme Court's recognition of paralegal tasks as: factual investigation, locating and interviewing witnesses, assistance with depositions, interrogatories, document production, compilation of statistical and financial data, checking legal citations, and drafting correspondence.[29]

Paralegal rates are appropriate when a task requires a paralegal's education, training, or experience. Their acquired knowledge enables them to exercise discretion in substantive legal work when supervised by an attorney who would otherwise perform the task.

WHAT IS THE ACTUAL VALUE OF A PARALEGAL'S SERVICES?

Lawyers spend years in law school, must pass a rigorous bar exam, and are licensed in the state where they practice before they can provide legal advice and charge professional fees. The national average billing rate for lawyers was $313 an hour in 2022.[30]

In contrast, paralegals earn an average wage of $30 an hour[31] yet their billing rates are often between $100 and $250, with larger firms often charging more. Unlike attorneys, paralegals are not required to be licensed in any state. Only

California requires individuals using the title "*paralegal*" to meet current and continuing education requirements.

While several states offer certification programs, these are voluntary. As a result, there can be a lack of oversight of a paralegal's qualifications when they charge $150 an hour to scan documents.

In a best-case scenario, a lawyer using a paralegal's services can devote more time to complex legal work. The qualified paralegal can then perform substantive legal tasks under proper supervision at a lower rate than the attorney would charge. In a worst-case scenario, clerical work is billed at a paralegal's rate, even though the tasks performed do not require paralegal training or expertise.

The fact that a person calls themselves a paralegal is not enough to justify a higher billing rate. Some courts have required evidence of a paralegal's qualifications before approving their charges. In fact, one court stated that payment for paralegal services should be supported by information regarding the paralegal's qualifications, acknowledgment that substantive work was performed under the direction and supervision of an attorney, and a description of the nature of the legal work.[32]

A lawyer can reduce a client's legal costs by effectively utilizing a paralegal, but this relationship can sometimes be abused. When reviewing your invoice, use this chapter to challenge the legitimacy of paralegal charges that may cross the line between compensable legal work and non-billable, non-legal tasks. Now is an excellent time to remind yourself of the importance of reviewing your fee agreement with your attorney before signing. Make sure that you did not unintentionally agree to pay for clerical tasks that an attorney might otherwise include in their office overhead.

The answer to the question posed at the beginning of this chapter is straightforward: a paralegal's obligation to bill responsibly is based on providing substantive legal work. The value of a paralegal should be based on the legal services they perform, and not on their job title or billing rate.

---

1. American Bar Association Standing Committee on Paralegals, *ABA Model Guidelines for the Utilization of Paralegal Services* (Chicago, Illinois: American Bar Association, 2018).
2. The National Federation of Paralegal Associations, *Model Code of Ethics and Professional Responsibility* (The National Federation of Paralegal Associations, 2016).
3. American Bar Association, "Current ABA Definition of Paralegal," accessed April 2, 2024.
4. *Missouri v. Jenkins*, 491 U.S. 274, 288 n.10 (1989).
5. *In re Olson*, 884 F.2d 1415 (D.C. Cir. 1989); *Cobell v. Norton*, 407 F. Supp. 2d 140 (D.D.C. 2005); *Precision Seed Cleaners v. Country Mut. Ins. Co.*, 976 F. Supp. 2d 1228 (D. Or. 2013); *Francis v. Atl. Infiniti, Ltd.*, 2012 N.Y. Slip Op. 50198 (N.Y. Sup. Ct. 2012).
6. *Salton Bay Marina, Inc. v. Imperial Irrigation Dist.*, 172 Cal.App.3d 914, 951 (Cal. Ct. App. 1985).
7. *Holladay v. Gestamp*, LLC, Dist. Court, ND Alabama 2025.
8. *Fierros v. Quebedeaux Buick GMC Inc.*, No. CV-20-00245-TUC-RM (MSA) (D. Ariz. 2021).

9. *Ridgeway v. Wal-Mart Stores Inc.*, 269 F. Supp. 3d 975, 991 (N.D. Cal. 2017).
10. *Hernandez v. Saybrook Buick GMC, Inc.*, No. 3:20-cv-00438 (VAB) (D. Conn. 2021).
11. *In re Orthopaedic Technology, Inc.*, 97 B.R. 596 (Bankr. D. Colo. 1989).
12. *Bratton v. Thomas Law Firm, PC,* 943 F. Supp. 2d 897 (N.D. Ind. 2013).
13. *Banks v. Dudek,* Dist. Court, WD Kentucky 2025.
14. *Charles v. LeBlanc,* Dist. Court, WD Louisiana 2025, Civil Action No. 18-0541.
15. *Bilazzo v. Portfolio Recovery Associates, LLC,* 876 F. Supp. 2d 452 (D.N.J. 2012).
16. *Lilly v. City of New York,* 934 F. 3d 222 - Court of Appeals, 2nd Circuit 2019.
17. *Young v. Spencer,* 405 P.3d 701 (Okla. Civ. App. 2017).
18. *Key Bank National Ass'n v. Van Noy,* 598 F. Supp. 2d 1160 (D. Or. 2009).
19. *Lewallen v. City of Beaumont,* Dist. Court, ED Texas 2009.
20. *North Coast Electric Co. v. Selig,* 151 P. 3d 211 (Wash. Ct. App. 2007).
21. *Miller v. Alamo,* 983 F.2d 856, 862 (8th Cir. 1993).
22. *Morris v. Belfor USA Group, Inc.,* 201 P. 3d 1253 - Colo: Court of Appeals, 7th Div. 2008.
23. *McMackin v. McMackin,* 651 A.2d 778 (Del. Fam. 1993).
24. *Taylor v. District of Columbia,* 325 F. Supp. 144 (D.D.C. 2018).
25. *State, Dept. of Transp. v. Skidmore,* 720 So. 2d 1125 (Fla. Dist. Ct. App. 1998).
26. *Spegon v. the Catholic Bishop of Chicago,* 175 F.3d 544 (7th Cir. 1999).

27. *Taylor v. Chubb Group of Ins. Companies,* 874 P.2d 806 (Okla. 1994).

28. *Gill Sav. Ass'n v. Int'l Supply Co.,* 759 S.W.2d 697, 702 (Tex. App.-Dallas. 1988, writ denied).

29. *Koontz v. Wells Fargo NA,* Dist. Court, SD West Virginia 2013.

30. Bieber, Christy, "How Much Do Lawyers Cost? 2023 Guide," *Forbes,* July 18, 2023.

31. U.S. Bureau of Labor Statistics, "Occupational Employment and Wage Statistics: Paralegals and Legal Assistants," April 25, 2023.

32. *El Apple I, Ltd. v. Olivas,* 370 SW 3d 757 - Tex: (Supreme Court 2012).

Chapter 6

HOW TO DISPUTE ATTORNEY FEES

Prepare your own legal fee audit.

The most cost-effective way to challenge unreasonable attorney fees is to conduct an audit. You'll begin by reviewing your invoice and identifying any charges that appear to be excessive, vague, or questionable. Using the information provided in this book, you'll learn how to document those entries and clearly explain why you believe they require further scrutiny. Once your attorney receives your audit, they become responsible for justifying the reasonableness of the disputed fees. If your attorney refuses to address the disputed charges, your completed audit provides a foundation for additional options. This chapter will guide you through the process of preparing your own attorney fee audit.

When facing a legal crisis that affects your family, home, or liberty, hiring an attorney can be a critical decision. Legal representation can be expensive, with rates ranging from $100 to more than $1,000 an hour. Realistically, the ability to pay legal fees may directly influence the quality of legal representation and, in some instances, the outcome of a case.

It is also concerning that the United States does not rank among the top ten countries in the World Justice Project Rule of Law Index,[1] which evaluates factors such as access to justice and the protection of fundamental rights. While no single ranking tells the entire story, it serves as a reminder that meaningful access to justice can be an ongoing challenge. By carefully reviewing attorney's fees, you can make informed decisions and better understand the value of your legal representation.

Let's assume you have just received your first legal invoice. You notice that the entire advance (retainer) has been depleted, there are charges for unknown services, and you are concerned about the amount of fees billed in just one month. As this guide points out, you recognize that an attorney has a fiduciary duty to charge fair and reasonable fees,[2] and you have a right to question the legitimacy of those fees without fear of retaliation.[3] By using well-supported, factual examples of potential overbilling as outlined in this guide, you may be able to resolve the fee issues found on the invoice with a simple, straightforward conversation with your attorney.

After reviewing the invoice, you become concerned that the charges do not appear to accurately reflect the legal services provided. For example, a paralegal billed $50 to schedule an appointment, an attorney charged $400 for a fifteen-minute meeting, and another paralegal billed $100 to copy a file. These are just a few examples from a three-page invoice. With an upcoming hearing, the unexpected fees understandably add to your stress.

So, how do you ensure that the attorney's billing practices are fair? Prepare an audit of the questionable fees and place the burden on the attorney to justify the charges. As mentioned earlier, legal auditors often assist large corporations by reviewing legal expenditures and detecting billing issues. However, it is not necessary to be a forensic accountant or a lawyer to challenge your own attorney's fees. With basic research and a careful review, you can identify potential issues on your legal invoice.

Alternatively, you could retain a legal fee auditor who will independently analyze the invoices to ensure accuracy. However, this book will help you prepare your own fee audit, as you may not have the desire or resources to hire third parties to dispute an attorney's fees.

The following is a step-by-step guide to preparing an audit of potentially unreasonable attorney fees. With an audit, you will have a discussion based on documented evidence instead of vague allegations. Additionally, the attorney's written response to your concerns can support the options explained in subsequent chapters.

PREPARE A LEGAL FEE AUDIT

1. Carefully review the invoice.
Compare your invoice to the fee agreement. Take the time to review each line to confirm that the hourly rates match those specified in the agreement. You can challenge any fees that are not in compliance.

Also, check the math. I once reviewed an invoice that accurately listed both the hourly rate and the time spent for each charge, but the total was mathematically incorrect. Apparently, a "surcharge" was added that was not stated in the fee agreement. Finally, make sure the review is timely, as some fee agreements impose deadlines for submitting written objections.

2. Identify potentially unreasonable fees.
Compare the charges on your invoice to the bill-padding practices described in Chapters 4 and 5. As you review each line of the invoice, flag any charges that seem excessive.

3. Document every questionable fee by listing:
* the date of service
* the task description (verbatim from the invoice)
* the person who performed the task
* the hourly rate billed
* the total fee charged for the task
* brief explanation for the dispute.

AUDIT TEMPLATE

INVOICE ANALYSIS: *Client* INV. # *1234* INV. DATE: *6/1/24* ABC LAW FIRM

DATE	DESCRIPTION of LEGAL SERVICE	ATTY HRS	RATE	STAFF HRS	RATE	AMOUNT	REASON for DISPUTE

4. Challenge fees with an audit

Organize the problematic fees in a clear and detailed format, as illustrated above. Provide a brief explanation for each disputed billing entry, using one or more of the 18 bill-padding examples discussed in this guide. Send a copy to your attorney and request a review of the questionable charges. A well-documented audit will effectively place the burden of justifying disputed fees on the attorney.

DISCUSS THE AUDIT WITH YOUR ATTORNEY

After completing the audit, you will be ready to challenge the disputed fees with your attorney. For many, this may be the most difficult step. You have trusted your attorney, and they may have supported you through tough times, but now you may feel disloyal raising concerns about their fees. These feelings are understandable, given the complex and often stressful circumstances you may find yourself in.

Reviewing and questioning problematic charges on your invoice is a sensible way of managing legal expenses and does not necessarily reflect a lack of trust in your attorney.

Contact the attorney's office and inform them that, after reviewing the latest invoice, you have questions. This initial discussion is critical because, at the very least, you will get a better understanding of your lawyer's integrity when you hear their reactions. Take notes and prepare a record of the attorney's responses. Your notes will be helpful for future reference or when drafting follow-up correspondence. A sample letter is provided on the next page.

If you have only one or two questions, a brief conversation with your attorney about the fees may resolve the matter. If you identify multiple issues, let the attorney know that you would like to send a list of the problems to their office for review. Your attorney may even suggest the same approach.

PUT YOUR CONCERNS IN WRITING

If you had a productive discussion with the attorney, and they explained the reasons for their billings, or made corrections, well done! Now, be sure to review each subsequent invoice promptly.

However, suppose you walk away from the conversation feeling that the attorney did not fully address your valid concerns. Or you may have more detailed questions that could not be answered during a phone call. In that case, the next step is to draft a letter describing your issues. Use the notes you took during your conversation as a guide. In the letter, be professional and unemotional, and rely on facts, not just opinions. This way, your comments will be taken seriously and will help maintain a constructive conversation. Several parties, including attorneys, arbitrators, and judges, may see this correspondence in the future. A letter that addresses specific issues found in the invoice is more productive than an emotional claim of "You cheated me." Treat the matter as a business dispute, and not a personal attack. Focus on the factual evidence, such as specific dates, amounts, and services listed in the audit. A sample letter is provided below for reference.

Dear Attorney,

As a follow-up to our recent discussion regarding Invoice #1234, dated May 1, 2025, I would like to provide additional information for your review. I've attached a spreadsheet identifying the specific charges we discussed, along with a brief explanation of my concerns.

For example, several clerical tasks billed on April 16 appear similar to entries billed on April 2. In addition, three entries dated April 8, 9, and 10 contain descriptions that are too vague for me to fully understand the legal work performed. I've also included several entries that are a bit confusing, and it would help if you could explain if and when these documents were filed.

Thank you. I appreciate your time and assistance in addressing these billing questions.

Sincerely,
Client

Your attorney should address the issues presented and provide a clear and appropriate explanation in response to your audit.

If this was the first invoice you received and you were able to resolve your billing concerns amicably, you're on your way to a productive relationship with your attorney. Addressing issues early helps establish expectations for future billing and encourages transparency from the outset.

Unfortunately, clients often wait until the end of their case to question their fees. Significant amounts of unpaid fees may have accumulated, unfavorable legal results might have occurred, and a feeling of mutual distrust has developed—not a very good scenario for you or your attorney. Nevertheless, the procedure is the same whether you start with the first invoice or question six months of accumulated legal bills. **Prepare your audit, contact the attorney, and put your concerns in writing.**

In the New York Times Bestseller, "*The (Honest) Truth about Dishonesty*,"[4] Author Dan Ariely mentions that supervision or even the "subtle suggestions of being watched can be effective in increasing honesty." This principle can be applied to the monitoring of your attorney's invoices. If your attorney knows you are carefully reviewing their invoices from the start, future disagreements can possibly be prevented. It takes little effort and only a brief lapse of conscience for an attorney to exaggerate billing hours while sitting alone in the office. Moreover, a lack of oversight of the legal fees on your invoice can unintentionally lead to questionable practices in the future due to the nature of hourly billing.

CAL'S CASE STUDY

This guide, so far, has explained how to identify and document problematic fees. The following case study practically applies these concepts by following a fictional client, Cal, who has just received his first legal invoice. With questions about potentially excessive fees, Cal drafted his own audit and outlined the reasons for each disputed fee to his attorney.

The following pages contain examples of billing entries drawn from actual invoices, slightly modified to preserve confidentiality. Unfortunately, Cal encountered multiple billing concerns during a single month. The individuals referenced in this case study are Ace (attorney), Barb (ex-wife), Cal (client), and Pen (paralegal). The final page of this chapter contains Cal's completed fee audit, which illustrates how the billing concerns discussed throughout the case study can be organized and documented.

Cal received his invoice on July 6, 2025, but failed to open his email until July 9. After reviewing the fee agreement, Cal noticed a clause that stated: "*If you fail to notify this firm in writing of any disputes relating to any charges on an invoice within 10 days of receipt, it is presumed that you agree the charges on the invoice are correct and fair.*"

Luckily, Cal recognized this important deadline and began drafting his audit. He examined every line item on the invoice and listed all the charges that appeared excessive. For each charge, he provided a reason for the dispute and entered the information into an audit template.

1. Lack of detail in describing attorney charges
05/01/25 REVIEW FILE 4.0 HOURS

Cal met with Ace, a divorce attorney, at the end of April. Ace did not charge Cal for the initial meeting, so Cal signed the fee agreement in his office after being served with paperwork by his ex-wife (Barb). Cal was overwrought in Ace's office and just wanted to respond to Barb's allegations. However, when Cal reviewed the fee charged by Ace on May 1, he felt it was excessive because there were not many documents to review. Cal also thought that the description of the charge failed to identify the documents that Ace reviewed. Cal challenged the fee because it did not provide enough information to support a claim for 4 hours of legal services.

...Because Ace was unable to explain why it took so long to review unnamed documents, he reduced the charge by 20%.

2. Lack of detail in describing staff charges
05/02/25 READ DOCUMENTS. 0.5 HOURS

Pen (the paralegal) billed Cal for reading documents that Ace had already reviewed. Pen did not specify the documents or the reason for reading them. Due to the vague description of the charges, evaluating the reasonableness of the fee became nearly impossible. Cal questioned Pen's fees because he didn't understand why the paralegal charged him for reading unnamed documents with no stated purpose.

...Pen stated she needed to review the documents to obtain addresses for future correspondence. She admitted this was a clerical task, so the charge was removed.

3. Billing expenses above cost
05/03/25 ATTORNEY SERVICE : RUSH

Cal identified an expense that seemed excessive. There was a $105 charge to file a simple substitution of attorney form. Cal was familiar with the procedure as he had previously represented himself in another case. Cal requested a receipt for the expense and found that an extra $20 had been added to the $25 cost of the *rush* service for no apparent reason. Cal found two problems with this charge. First, there was no justification for paying extra for the rush service, as the filing was timely, and there were no circumstances that called for the additional $20 upcharge.

...Ace removed the $20 upcharge from the invoice and reduced the costs by an additional $25 for the unnecessary "rush" service.

4. Billing for tasks not performed.
05/04/25 PREPARE AND FILE MOTION 3.0 HOURS

On May 4, Ace billed 3 hours for a motion that Cal didn't recognize. The title of the motion was not provided, and Cal never received a copy. Cal challenged this fee because he had no evidence that it had ever been prepared.

...Ace admitted this charge was billed in error and deducted the fee from the invoice.

5. Block billing
05/05/25 EMAIL, CONFERENCE, REVIEW FILE, RESEARCH, DRAFT DOCS, MEETING, CALL 4.5 HOURS

On May 5, Ace combined several separate tasks and charged a single fee. The description included phone calls, emails, research, a conference, and drafting tasks. Cal felt it was impossible to figure out the reasonableness of each charge. Cal researched the term block billing and found that it is a widespread practice that warrants scrutiny. Cal believes he has a right to understand what work was performed and the cost of every legal service provided to him.

...Ace separated the block billing charge into individual tasks and reduced the fee by 20%.

6. Clerical tasks billed at a paralegal rate
05/06/25 EMAIL CLIENT COPY OF LETTER 0.2 HOURS

Pen emailed a copy of a letter to Cal, and charged a paralegal rate for the work. Cal questioned this fee because copying and emailing a letter does not involve substantial legal work and does not require advanced education or experience. A clerk or secretary could have performed this task, which is typically included in the attorney's overhead. There was no reason for Pen to charge a fee for this task.

...Ace deducted this fee from the invoice.

7. Clerical/Paralegal tasks billed at an attorney's rate
05/07/25 FILE COMPLAINT WITH COURT 0.3 HOURS

Ace was in the courthouse on May 7, so he filed his own pleadings with the court. Filing pleadings is undoubtedly an acceptable task for an attorney. However, Cal believed that an attorney should not charge an attorney's rate for performing paralegal or clerical tasks. He contacted Ace's office to request clarification regarding what he considered an excessive fee.

...Ace changed the hourly rate for the filing fee task from an attorney's rate to the paralegal's rate.

8. Charges related to billing
05/08/25 CALL TO CLIENT RE: INVOICE. 0.3 HOURS

Cal contacted Ace's office in early May and asked how much he would be charged for Ace filing the Substitution of Attorney. Pen answered the call and charged Cal for the conversation, which is unusual as clients typically aren't charged for billing inquiries. Cal thought it was odd to be charged for a non-legal billing question, so he included this fee to his audit.

...Ace subsequently deducted this charge from the invoice.

9. Chipping
05/09/25 CONFERENCE, PREPARE LETTER, EMAIL LETTER, SCAN EMAIL TO FILE TOTAL 1.0 HOUR

Pen billed 0.4 hours to prepare a cover letter. She also billed three separate 0.2-hour minimum charges: one for emailing the letter, one for scanning the letter, and another for an unspecified conference. Cal thought that charging the minimum for simple, quick tasks was excessive, so he asked Pen why these minor tasks were each billed separately.

...Pen explained that she was permitted to charge a minimum of 0.2 hours for tasks under the terms of the fee agreement and declined to adjust the charges. Cal felt uneasy with her explanation, but understood that he had signed the agreement. Even so, he was uncomfortable with the office policy of applying the minimum increment to such small tasks.

10. Churning
05/10/25 EX PARTE HEARING. 2.0 HOURS

An issue arose when Barb failed to return their child's clothes to Cal after visitation. Ace recommended an emergency hearing. Cal, angry over the incident, felt that a phone call could possibly resolve the matter, but he accepted his attorney's advice. Ace prepared the paperwork, filed an ex parte motion, and appeared in court. However, the judge denied the frivolous motion because it was clearly not an emergency and ordered Cal to pay Barb's attorney fees.

...Cal disputed the fees for the pointless hearing based on the judge's ruling. Ace told Cal that he couldn't expect to win every time in court and refused to delete the charge. It seemed to Cal that Ace performed an unnecessary legal service, resulting in inflated fees. At this point, Cal began to question Ace's billing practices.

11. Duplicate billing
05/11/25 PREPARE LETTER TO CLIENT. 0.4 HOURS

On May 11, Pen billed Cal for the same letter that had been billed on May 9. Cal contacted Pen and reminded her that he had already been billed for this service. After reviewing the file, Pen acknowledged that they had just switched to a new billing system. She told Cal she would review the file and get back to him. On a later call, Pen admitted it was an error caused by the new billing system.

...Pen acknowledged that it was a legitimate error and deleted the charge.

12. Excessive entries for document review
5/12, 5/14, 5/18, 5/21/25. REVIEW DOCUMENTS 8.0 HOURS

As Cal continued to review every line item on the invoice, he identified four separate charges for document review. Ace had already billed him for reviewing the materials provided during their first meeting, but Cal knew a hearing might be approaching. Still, he was confused about which documents were being reviewed and why so many reviews were necessary. He noticed that all of the charges had been rounded to the nearest hour. Given the number of review entries in a relatively short period, Cal felt Ace should provide more detailed billing descriptions.

...Cal eventually questioned these fees during arbitration, and they were reduced by 25%.

13. Excessive time for legal research
05/18/25 RESEARCH. 4.0 HOURS

Cal reviewed the $1,600 charge for legal research and didn't understand why it was so expensive. Cal was not a lawyer and wasn't sure how to challenge this fee. However, Cal felt that Ace should provide a more detailed description of the legal research that was performed. Cal did know that if he asked Ace for clarification, it would become the attorney's responsibility to support the four hours spent on research.

Ace eventually reduced the fee because he discovered that a portion of the hours spent on research was duplicated due to the new billing system. As a result, Cal's skepticism about the excessive charge was justified, but at a cost. Because of this error, along with numerous others, Cal continued to lose faith in the attorney.

...During arbitration, this fee was reduced by $400.

14. Excessive time to complete a task
05/18/25 PREPARE PROOF OF SERVICE 1.0 HOURS

Pen charged Cal for preparing a one-page proof of service. Since Cal had previously represented himself, he was familiar with the document and believed it should not take an hour to complete. Cal recognized that it can be very difficult, if not impossible, for someone without legal training to determine if the time billed for preparing legal documents is reasonable. However, Cal knew there were a few reasonably simple documents that he could address.

So Cal asked why it took so long to prepare a simple document. Cal inquired about the fee in a businesslike manner. In response, Pen acknowledged that there were no unusual issues involved in preparing the document and explained that the excessive fee resulted from a typographical error. The charge should have been 0.1 hours, not 1 hour. Cal learned that even an unintentional billing error, if left unaddressed, can be costly.

...The fee was reduced from $150 to $15.

15. Fees not in compliance with the retainer agreement
5/20/25 TELEPHONE CALL TO COURT 0.2 HOURS

At the end of the month, Ace increased the paralegal's hourly rate to $175. Cal reviewed the fee agreement and confirmed Pen's rate was $150 per hour. Cal also confirmed that Ace had not provided advance notice of Pen's increased rate. Without warning, Cal was charged a higher rate he neither anticipated nor agreed to. The unexpected fee increase not only affected Cal's financial planning but also added to his trust issues with Ace.

...Cal contacted Ace and informed him of the agreed-upon rate of $150 an hour. Ace changed the hourly rate back to $150 and then advised Cal that Pen's rate would increase to $175 the following month.

16. High minimum increments
05/22/25 TELEPHONE CALL 0.3 HOURS

Ace charged 0.3 of an hour for a two-minute phone call to the opposing counsel. He appropriately billed for 2 minutes of phone time, but due to the minimum billing increment, an additional 16 minutes were automatically added to the charge. Cal's fee agreement clearly identified Ace's minimum billing as 0.3 of an hour, an increment generally considered excessive. Since Cal had already agreed to the high minimum in the original fee agreement, there was little recourse except to ask the attorney about the "phantom" 16 minutes billed for no apparent legal task.

Cal later researched the issue and found that attorneys sometimes provide a rationale for such high minimums by suggesting that a lot of work goes into making a telephone call. However, Cal was not convinced and decided that high minimum increments could be viewed as billing for work not performed if an adequate explanation is not provided for the "phantom" minutes.

...Ace refused to reduce the fee because he said the minimum billing increment had been clearly stated in the fee agreement. Cal then realized that during their first meeting, he had been so emotional that he hadn't carefully reviewed the fee agreement before signing it.

17. Rounded time estimates
05/25/25 PREPARE FOR TRIAL 8 HOURS

As Ace prepared for trial, he performed numerous tasks but failed to provide adequate information about them. Ace billed $3,200 for eight hours of work with the simple description: "*Prepare for Trial.*" Cal objected to this charge, even though he understood that a meticulously detailed listing of every task was not required. However, Cal felt that a better description could help him feel assured that the fees were reasonable. Cal also researched the issue of rounded hours and found the practice to be a red flag, as there was once again not enough information to determine the accuracy of the fees.

...Cal addressed the fee during arbitration, and Ace voluntarily reduced it by $1200.

18. Vague descriptions
05/25/25 PREPARE FOR DISCOVERY. 3.0 HOURS

During Cal's first meeting with his attorney, they discussed case strategy. Ace felt there was no need for discovery at that time. As a result, when Cal received the invoice, there was a $1,200 charge that immediately struck Cal as questionable because the task description, "Prepare for discovery," was so vague as to raise suspicions. When Cal questioned Ace about the charge, the attorney was unable to produce evidence of discovery preparations.

Cal had no legal background and recognized that he was at a disadvantage when faced with legal bills described in ambiguous terms. But Cal recognized that vague descriptions had been a significant issue with Ace's hourly billings.

Cal concluded that he could no longer trust his attorney due to the significant number of billing errors. He terminated their relationship and retained new counsel. Both Cal and Ace learned the importance of billing transparency: upholding the ethical standards of the legal profession preserves a client's trust and confidence. Additionally, Cal learned the importance of thoroughly reading his fee agreement before signing it.

Cal and Ace ultimately ended up in arbitration because the fee agreement required all disputes to be resolved through binding arbitration. Using his fee audit, Cal challenged the disputed charges and successfully reduced his legal fees.

The examples and case studies in this chapter are illustrative and based on a compilation of real-world billing disputes. Names, details, and outcomes have been modified for educational purposes. Descriptions of conduct that reflect client concerns, dispute outcomes, or judicial findings are not intended to characterize the conduct of any individual attorney.

WHAT HAPPENS IF YOUR ATTORNEY REFUSES TO ADDRESS THE DISPUTED FEES?

In this case study, Cal was required to participate in binding arbitration for a fee dispute under the terms of his fee agreement. Your response to a fee dispute may also depend upon the terms of your own fee agreement. If you have provided a copy of your audit to your attorney, but they either refuse to discuss or address the challenged fees, you've reached an escalated stage of the dispute process.

You might decide to accept potentially excessive legal bills and do nothing because you're worried about the consequences of confronting your attorney. Or you could formally address your disputed fees, which may unfortunately lead to an adversarial relationship. Either way, subsequent actions become more stressful and expensive.

Too many clients face this dilemma when they discover substantial billing errors. There is no fairy-tale ending to this chapter, no magic wand to wipe away the financial hardship of excessive fees. However, there are alternative ways to address unreasonable fees if your attorney refuses to address your questions. The escalated procedures available to dispute fees include filing a state bar complaint, mediation, arbitration, or a civil lawsuit.

If you have drafted your own fee audit and have documented evidence of potentially excessive fees, you are ready to take the next step. Logically, no-cost options are the first place to start. Filing a state bar complaint for professional misconduct based on unreasonable fees will require effort on your part, but there should be no financial obligations involved. Free mediation or arbitration services might be offered by the bar organization in your state, but may still require legal assistance and additional expenses, especially if you are not familiar with the process. The following two chapters will explain each of these options in detail.

Whether you have accumulated a substantial fee balance at the end of your case or have an ongoing relationship with an attorney, you can still avoid an Attorney Fee Hustle.

---

1. World Justice Project, "Global Scores & Rankings."
2. *Bird v. Superior Court*, 130 Cal. Rptr. 2d 782 (Cal. Ct. App. 2003).
3. American Bar Association, "Rule 8.4: Misconduct" in Model Rules of Professional Conduct, 2020.
4. Ariely, Dan, *The (Honest) Truth about Dishonesty: How We Lie to Everyone--Especially Ourselves* (New York: Harper Perennial, 2013).

CAL'S ATTORNEY FEE AUDIT

INVOICE ANALYSIS: **<u>CAL</u>** **INVOICE # 123** **DATE June 30, 2025**

	DATE	ITEM DESCRIPTION	ATTY HRS	ATTY RATE	PARA HRS	PARA RATE	CHARGE	REASON FOR DISPUTE
1	05/01/25	Review file	4.0	$400			$1,600	*Lack of detail for attorney charges*
2	05/02/25	Read documents			0.5	$150	$75	*Lack of detail for staff charges*
3	05/03/25	Attorney Service: Rush					$105	*Billing expenses above cost*
4	05/04/25	Prepare and file motion	3.0	$400			$1,200	*No record of motion or filing*
5	05/05/25	Email to client; conf with paralegal, review file, legal research, draft docs, meeting with opp counsel, call client	4.5				$1,800	*Block billing*
6	05/06/25	Email client copy of letter from OC			0.2	$150	$30	*Clerical tasks billed at paralegal rate*
7	05/07/25	File complaint with the court	0.3	$400			$120	*Paralegal tasks charged at an atty rate*
8	05/08/25	Telephone call/ client re: invoice			0.3	$150	$45	*Charges related to billing*
9	05/09/25	Conference with attorney			0.2	$150	$30	*Chipping*
9	05/09/25	Prepare letter to client re: meeting			0.4	$150	$60	*Chipping*
9	05/09/25	Email letter to client			0.2	$150	$30	*Chipping*
9	05/09/25	Scan email to file			0.2	$150	$30	*Chipping*
10	05/10/25	Exparte hearing re: visitation	2	$400			$800	*Churning*
11	05/11/25	Prepare letter to client re: meeting			0.4	$150	$60	*Duplicate billing*
12	05/12/25	Review documents	2	$400			$800	*Excessive entries for document review*
12	05/14/25	Review documents	1	$400			$400	*Excessive entries for document review*
12	05/18/25	Review documents	3	$400			$1,200	*Excessive entries for document review*
12	05/21/25	Review documents	2	$400			$800	*Excessive entries for document review*
13	05/18/25	Research	4	$400			$1,600	*Excessive legal research: lack of detail*
14	05/18/25	Prepare proof of service			1.0	$150	$150	*Excessive time to complete a task*
15	05/20/25	Telephone call to court re: hearing			0.2	$175	$35	*Fees not in compliance with rertainer*
16	05/22/25	Telephone call to OC re: hearing	0.3	$400			$120	*High minimum increments*
17	05/25/25	Prepare for trial	8	$400			$3,200	*Rounded time estimates; vague*
18	05/25/25	Prepare for discovery	3	$400			$1,200	*Vague description*

CHAPTER 7
STATE BAR COMPLAINT

Attorneys are fiduciaries.

"Attorneys are fiduciaries. As such, they must expend client resources prudently to serve the best interests of the client, not the attorney."[1] Moreover, because the legal profession is self-governing, it bears a continuing responsibility to ensure that its rules serve the public interest rather than the interests of the profession itself.[2]

Due to these high standards, if you are unable to resolve an unreasonable fee dispute directly with your attorney, an available option to consider is filing an ethical misconduct complaint. This chapter provides a general overview of the complaint process. If you decide to move forward, the rules for each state can be found on their respective websites – Chapter 10 provides specific contact information for every state.

Note: This option may present challenges due to the self-governing nature of attorney discipline and may require persistence. Even so, clients are entitled to raise concerns regarding unreasonable billing practices, and bar associations have a responsibility to take those concerns seriously. You should not be forced to incur additional expenses simply to seek accountability for alleged ethical violations.

WHY FILE A COMPLAINT WITH A STATE BAR ASSOCIATION?

There are two main reasons for filing an ethical complaint against your attorney for unreasonable fees: accountability and cost. First, attorneys should be held accountable for excessive charges that violate their professional standards. Intentional overbilling is a breach of trust and warrants serious consequences. Second, clients should not bear the expense of resolving ethical issues. Allegations of bill padding supported by credible evidence deserve access to the same cost-free disciplinary process available for other ethical complaints.

Filing a complaint with a state bar association for unreasonable fees is a practical choice if your attorney refuses to address documented overbilling. However, it is important to take steps to ensure that the state bar handles your complaint correctly. One legal authority has cautioned,

"Clients derive so little from the process that it is surprising that they bother filing complaints at all."[3]

Let's assume you have prepared and submitted your fee audit to your attorney. But the attorney refuses to address the alleged overbilling, and your attempt to informally resolve the matter fails. In this situation, you may want to consider contacting your state bar association or the disciplinary agency that oversees attorney conduct. Note: The term "bar" originates from the physical divider in a courtroom separating the public from court officials, and also refers to the legal profession as a whole.

Each state bar's website provides important information to consider when filing an ethical complaint for unreasonable fees. Remember, it is professional misconduct for an attorney to charge an unreasonable fee,[4] but the "ultimate authority over the legal profession is vested largely in the courts."[5] And since courts are comprised of members of the legal profession, self-regulation raises its own set of concerns.

One of those concerns is that some bar associations tend to view an unreasonable fee dispute as a contractual rather than an ethical issue. A number of state bar associations divert complaints involving unreasonable fees into proceedings that may require additional financial investment for professional advice or advocacy. By treating all fee disputes as contractual matters, state bars often complicate and increase the expense of addressing complaints about unethical fees. Certain states offer no-cost mediation or arbitration, but these options still leave a non-lawyer at a distinct disadvantage.

Meanwhile, all other misconduct complaints alleging an attorney's ethical violations are investigated at no cost to clients. Complaints involving unreasonable fees should be handled in exactly the same way. Clients deserve a cost-free process for filing a complaint when an attorney violates their ethical duty to charge a reasonable fee. However, it is important to understand the obstacles you might face. First and foremost is the definition of what constitutes an unreasonable fee. A client questioning potentially unethical fees should be able to rely on the state bar to regulate the fee dispute process fairly, but ***how can fairness be assured if unreasonable fees are so difficult to define?***

WHAT IS AN UNREASONABLE FEE?

Chapter 4 presents 18 examples of hourly billing practices that state and federal courts have found to be unacceptable. Numerous law journals and legal texts have discussed these same bill-padding tactics, recognizing that they can artificially inflate legal fees. A straightforward definition of unreasonable is "not fair, sensible, or appropriate."[6] Nevertheless, some bar associations continue to struggle with distinguishing unreasonable fees from ordinary contractual fee disputes.

Here is one legal definition of an unreasonable fee: "A fee is excessive when, after a review of the facts, a lawyer of ordinary prudence would be left with a definite and firm conviction that the fee is in excess of a reasonable fee."[7] In other words, a fee is excessive when an attorney has a definite conviction it is excessive? Unfortunately, this definition is not very transparent. Relying on an attorney's "conviction" does not help a *client* evaluate billing discrepancies. What process does an attorney use and what facts are needed for an attorney to make that judgment? Is the lack of clarity in defining reasonable fees intentional? Without clear guidelines, it becomes difficult for clients to hold attorneys accountable for unethical billing practices. State bar courts have also faced challenges in defining a reasonable fee. As one court notes, "[F]ew, if any, areas of attorney discipline are as subject to differing interpretations as the matter of what constitutes an excessive attorney's fee."[8]

Despite this confusion, there are two indisputable principles: attorneys have a fiduciary duty to act in their clients best interests and an ethical obligation to charge reasonable fees.

To analyze unreasonable fees, the ABA has formalized factors[9] that courts have used to address the issue:
(1) the time and labor required, the novelty and difficulty of the questions involved, and the skill requisite to perform the legal service properly;
(2) the likelihood, if apparent to the client, that the acceptance of the particular employment will preclude other employment by the lawyer;
(3) the fee customarily charged in the locality for similar legal services;
(4) the amount involved and the results obtained;
(5) the time limitations imposed by the client or by the circumstances;
(6) the nature and length of the professional relationship with the client;

(7) the experience, reputation, and ability of the lawyer or lawyers performing the services; and
(8) whether the fee is fixed or contingent.

Note that the ABA factors do not use clear, definitive language, such as block billing, ambiguous task descriptions, high minimum increments, or improper charges for clerical tasks. One legal article noted: "[T]he test employed by the ABA codes to measure reasonableness is so vague that it is virtually useless."[10]

However, in California, the State Bar recently replaced and superseded its Arbitration Advisory for determining a reasonable fee.[11] The advisory is now 27 pages long and outlines 13 unconscionability factors, as well as 28 relevant questions to consider in a reasonable fee analysis. Notably, the advisory points out that determining a reasonable fee involves assessing the "adequacy of the attorney's time records" and refers explicitly to block billing as a questionable practice. Even so, clients disputing fees in any state must be able to identify potential errors within an attorney's records to ensure discrepancies are properly addressed.

THE CHALLENGE

Without formal training, clients are often placed in a difficult position in a fee dispute. They are expected to interpret vague definitions and complex factors to provide a nuanced legal analysis of the reasonableness of an attorney's fees. In other words, you are expected to be an attorney or hire one to resolve your attorney's questionable billing practices, even though, as a fiduciary, "It remains the lawyer's burden to prove the value of the legal services rendered."[12]

But does it make sense to require a legal expert to determine that it is unreasonable for an attorney's paralegal to bill $150 an hour to download documents? Or is litigation required to prove an attorney violated ethical rules by billing three hours of their time at $400 per hour, for a total of $1,200, for a document they never prepared? Or is it necessary to go through all the ABA's factors to decide the unreasonableness of $935,000 in fees charged by an attorney on two invoices, "with all of her time entry descriptions limited to either 'strategy' or 'factual analysis' without further elaboration?" (The last example was found on legal invoices submitted as Exhibit 3 in Case No. CGC-23-607461, Plaintiff X, formerly known as Twitter vs. Wachtell, Lipton, Rosen & Katz.)

In the fifth edition of an ABA Law Practice Management text, the following question is posed: "How do you know what's reasonable?" The answer is straightforward: "No formula answers that question."[13]

It is essential to remember that, despite all the legal rhetoric, unreasonable fees are unethical and dishonest.

This guide helps decode the mystery of "unreasonable fees" by providing practical tools and real-world examples that will enable clients to effectively monitor their legal bills. When documented evidence of potential overbilling is presented to an attorney, it becomes their responsibility to justify the charges.

If the attorney fails to address a client's questions adequately, the self-regulating legal profession should resolve unreasonable fee disputes at no additional cost to the client to correct the ethical confusion it has created.

In my first year practicing family law, several clients shared invoices from their former attorneys. They were frustrated as they pointed out what they believed were excessive fees that their previous attorneys had brushed off without explanation. As I reviewed the bills, I noticed the same troubling patterns: block-billed entries, vague descriptions, and excessive charges for clerical and secretarial work.

I encouraged these clients to bring their questions to the state bar, but the responses they received were discouraging. The complaints were seen as simple fee disagreements, so no disciplinary action was taken. These cases introduced me to the challenges clients face when seeking help with unreasonable fees. The organizations that regulate attorneys may, in fact, downplay the impact of such complaints.

HOW DO ETHICAL RULES AFFECT AN ATTORNEY'S OBLIGATION TO CHARGE REASONABLE FEES?

An attorney is a fiduciary, meaning his relationship with you requires "absolute and perfect candor, openness and honesty, and the absence of any concealment or deception."[14] Additionally, the attorney has the burden of proving that the fees they charge are reasonable.[15] Every state has adopted attorney ethics rules derived from the ABA Model Rules of Professional Conduct, although each jurisdiction modifies the rules to accommodate its own laws and policies.

Rule 1.5 states, "A lawyer shall not make an agreement for, charge, or collect an unreasonable fee or an unreasonable amount for expenses."

Rule 8.4 states, "It is professional misconduct for a lawyer to violate the Rules of Professional Conduct or to engage in conduct involving dishonesty, fraud, deceit or misrepresentation."

These rules clearly establish unreasonable fees as **professional misconduct.** When state bar associations adopted the ABA model rules, several replaced the term "unreasonable" with alternatives such as "clearly excessive," "unconscionable," "illegal," "excessive," or "prohibited." Despite the different wording, each term upholds the same principle: unreasonable fees are unethical and violate the legal profession's code of conduct.

A viable course of action for clients dealing with unreasonable fees is to turn to the agency responsible for enforcing an attorney's ethical obligations – the state bar association. If you have documented examples of your attorney padding their bill and refusing to resolve questionable charges, filing a complaint with the state bar can be the best way to resolve your dispute because of the profession's ethical standards.

"[T]he fundamental purpose of disciplinary proceedings is to maintain the integrity of the legal profession, to protect the administration of justice from reproach, and to safeguard the public."[16]

Unfortunately, some state bar associations sometimes forget this mission and treat unreasonable fee complaints differently from other disciplinary complaints.

INTENTIONAL OVERBILLING: PROFESSIONAL MISCONDUCT OR A FEE DISPUTE?

Considering the consequences, the differences between a professional misconduct complaint and a fee dispute are substantial.

A professional misconduct complaint (or grievance) against an attorney is a very serious charge. Examples include: conflicts of interest, violations of client confidentiality, neglect of client matters, or charging unreasonable fees. All of these ethical violations are subject to sanctions under a state bar's disciplinary process, which can result in private reprimands, public reprovals, probation with or without suspension, and, in extreme cases, disbarment. Every state bar provides information on how to file an ethical complaint against an attorney, and there is typically no cost to file the complaint.

A contractual fee dispute between an attorney and a client involves the failure of one of the parties to comply with the terms of their agreement. For instance, a client may not comply with a provision requiring payment of an invoice within thirty days, or an attorney may refuse to refund the unused portion of a retainer, despite specific wording in the agreement. These types of contractual fee issues are often resolved through mediation or arbitration, and a client might even consider the costs of pursuing a lawsuit. However, these are the expected consequences of addressing a breach of contract claim.

A fee dispute with allegations of bill padding or intentional overbilling goes beyond a simple contractual disagreement. The ABA's Model Rules of Professional Conduct prohibit attorneys from charging unreasonable fees, and alleged violations of these ethical rules should be investigated as ethical complaints, at no cost to the client. Yet some state bar associations fail to clearly distinguish between contractual disagreements and ethics violations by providing confusing or inconsistent guidance on how to challenge *unreasonable* fees.

This lack of clarity leaves clients struggling to navigate the system and can result in additional and unnecessary expenses. When bar associations fail to provide clear guidelines for challenging unreasonable fees, they undermine the integrity of the legal profession and neglect their duty to protect the public.

WHEN DOES A FEE DISPUTE TURN INTO AN ETHICS VIOLATION?

A fee dispute with clear evidence of intentional overbilling is much more than a contractual disagreement. If an attorney bills for work that was not performed or repeatedly exaggerates the time spent on legal tasks, those billing practices violate both the attorney's ethical and fiduciary duties.

To effectively address cases of intentional overbilling, state bar associations need to clearly distinguish between routine contractual fee disagreements and unethical charges that should be handled as professional misconduct complaints. Without clear guidance, clients attempting to resolve unethical fees are often directed to file a standard fee disagreement, which may not address the misconduct involved.

It is essential to understand that fee disputes involving unreasonable fees can be pursued as a professional misconduct complaint because charging unreasonable fees violates an attorney's code of conduct.

When you first review a state bar's website, you'll likely see two separate sections: fee disputes and attorney complaints (grievances). A common mistake clients make is following the instructions for fee disputes when their issues involve intentional overbilling or bill padding, issues better suited for a misconduct complaint.

Unfortunately, some state bar disciplinary procedures may discourage clients from filing ethical complaints about unreasonable fees by presenting confusing information that directs individuals toward mediation or arbitration. To maintain the profession's integrity, bar associations responsible for governing attorney conduct should streamline the process of handling complaints related to unreasonable fees. Instead, they use questionable logic to differentiate between fee disputes and other professional misconduct complaints, relying on a commonly held rationale that fee disputes do not involve ethical issues.

The following are examples of how some state bar associations treat fee disputes:

"Fee disputes usually do not involve issues of professional misconduct."[17]

"Except for unusual circumstances, a disagreement over legal fees is not evidence of misconduct."[18]

"The State Bar doesn't oversee how much an attorney can charge consumers."[19]

If bar associations structure systems that give *attorneys* an advantage by assuming that fee disputes do not involve misconduct, the victims of **unreasonable hourly fees** are burdened with unnecessary barriers to resolving their disputes.

This assumption makes it more difficult for the client to file a complaint and conflicts with the legal profession's responsibility "to ensure its regulations are in the public's interest and not their own."[20]

When you challenge the reasonableness of an attorney's fees, the burden should be on the attorney, as a fiduciary, to establish their entitlement to the amount charged.[21]

ASSERT YOUR RIGHT TO FILE A COMPLAINT FOR UNREASONABLE FEES.

While some bar associations clearly outline how to file a complaint for unethical fees, others make the fee dispute process confusing, potentially leading you into more complex legal actions, which could require hiring yet another attorney. Although every bar association states that unreasonable (unconscionable, excessive, illegal, etc.) fees are unethical, you may have to assert your right to file an ethical complaint by emphasizing that you have documented evidence of potential bill-padding.

To identify potential roadblocks that might interfere with filing a complaint against an attorney for professional misconduct due to unreasonable fees, I contacted the bar associations of the three states with the largest number of attorneys: New York, California, and Texas. The combined total of lawyers in these three states comprises 27% of the nation's lawyers.[22] Yet their websites do not provide clear instructions on how to dispute cases involving an attorney's ***unreasonable fees.***

The New York State Bar Website[23] initially has separate instructions for fee disputes and attorney misconduct claims. To the client, it may not be clear that a fee dispute due to *overbilling or bill padding* can be treated as an attorney grievance.

The State Bar of Texas Bar Website[24] states that its attorney grievance system cannot solve a fee dispute.

The State Bar of California Website[25] states that they do not "oversee how much an attorney can charge consumers. But if you feel that your bill is too high, you can ask for Fee Arbitration to resolve the dispute."

When I contacted the State Bars of New York and Texas, I asked if I could file a complaint (grievance) with the bar association if I had evidence of overbilling. Both states immediately stated that I could. I was directed to their online complaint forms.

When I called the California State Bar, I asked about filing a complaint for overbilling. I was told that fee disputes are usually directed to arbitration. However, after I explained my concern about bill padding, I was informed that I could file an ethics complaint, and a state bar investigator would decide whether to proceed with the complaint or refer the dispute to arbitration.

All three websites address fee disputes and attorney ethical complaints as separate and distinct actions, yet when questioned, all three associations stated that I could file an ethical complaint for **unreasonable** fees. ***The lesson learned is that you must assert your right to file a misconduct complaint for unethical fees.***

This book focuses on the relevant percentage of clients with legitimate complaints about unethical hourly billing practices. Research suggests that overbilling and bill padding are *not* that uncommon. According to a California State Bar Arbitration Advisory, block billing may inflate legal bills by 10-30%.[26] An ABA article reported a survey indicating that

21% of lawyers overcharged their hourly clients by rounding up the number of hours.[27] A recent audit showed that out of 800 West Virginia attorneys billing for court-appointed work, approximately 100 were found to be overbilling. One West Virginia attorney admitted to billing more than 24 hours a day multiple times.[28]

Despite these compelling statistics, some bar associations continue to treat fee disputes for unreasonable fees with seemingly less interest than other ethical complaints. A state bar or its judiciary takes complaints of professional misconduct seriously and typically covers the costs of the proceedings. However, a dispute involving unreasonable fees may seem less important because the cost shifts to you, the client.

If you cannot resolve an unreasonable fee dispute directly with your attorney, you may be forced into a system that immediately puts you at a disadvantage. Even with no-cost mediation or arbitration, representing yourself against an attorney can be difficult. You would be well advised to seek legal counsel, which, of course, means an additional expense.

However, there is an option, an alternative action for challenging unreasonable attorney fees: file a professional misconduct complaint, along with a request for restitution, as explained in this chapter.

REQUEST RESTITUTION FOR UNETHICAL FEES

When you file a misconduct complaint (also referred to as a grievance) against your attorney for charging unreasonable fees in violation of ethical rules, you should specifically request restitution for any excessive amounts you paid. Because many state bar associations fail to draw a clear distinction between unethical billing practices and ordinary fee disputes, they may decline to address restitution or refuse to order it altogether. Although charging unreasonable fees is considered unethical in every state, a client's ability to recover excessive charges varies significantly from one jurisdiction to another.

The following are examples of states that acknowledge the problem of unethical fees and actually explain the difference between normal fee disagreements and unreasonable fee disputes.

"The grievance process is an investigation to decide if an attorney is guilty of misconduct. In some cases, the committee can order the attorney to pay you restitution."[29]

"In some cases, however, such as when the fee charged is either illegal or clearly excessive, ethics are involved. In those cases where the lawyer is found to be at fault, discipline will follow."[30]

"Sometimes a bar member's fees violate the rules of professional conduct. In these cases, the member may be disciplined. More often, however, clients believe the fees are not reasonable because they lost their case or because they feel their lawyer did a poor job representing them."[31]

"We may initiate an investigation into a lawyer's fee if the fee charged or the fee agreement is improper under the ethics rules. Many fee-related complaints, however, stem from general dissatisfaction with the amount of fees charged for legal services that may not have achieved the client's legal objectives. These situations ordinarily do not provide a basis for possible disciplinary charges."[32]

But other states tell you outright that fee disputes are not handled by the disciplinary process or that you should not expect a refund.

"Please note that filing a Bar complaint is not a proper or likely way to obtain a refund or monetary damages."[33]

"Filing a grievance triggers an initial review by our intake unit to determine if the grievance contains allegations of unethical conduct." But, "The Office of Disciplinary Counsel does not refund the fees you have paid to an attorney."[34]

"Fee disputes are not normally handled within the attorney disciplinary process. Individuals should pursue fee disputes with the Bar association in the county where the attorney practices."[35]

"You should not expect to receive a refund of fees as a result of filing a grievance. Discuss your concerns about fees with your lawyer. For information about dispute resolution centers..."[36]

If you live in a state that does not offer restitution for unreasonable fees, you face a much more difficult challenge, especially if there is no ability to address unreasonable fee disputes through the attorney disciplinary process. Clients *and* attorneys would benefit if bar associations made it easier to address unreasonable fees. Clients deserve the opportunity to resolve unethical overbilling without the added stress and financial burden of another lawsuit. At the same time, attorneys would gain a better understanding that charging unreasonable hourly fees carries consequences just as serious as other forms of professional misconduct. To effectively proceed with an ethical complaint for unreasonable fees, you'll first have to understand what your state bar offers in resolving fee disputes at no cost, assert your right to dispute unethical fees, and request an order for restitution.

HOW TO FILE A COMPLAINT FOR PROFESSIONAL MISCONDUCT DUE TO UNREASONABLE FEES

Consider the following suggestions if you decide to file an ethical complaint against your attorney for unreasonable fees:

1. Your initial contact with the state bar should be a fact-finding telephone call. Let them know you have documented evidence of potential bill padding and overbilling.

2. Explain that you believe you have evidence of the attorney potentially violating either ABA Ethics Rule 1.5 (an attorney shall not charge an excessive fee) or ABA Ethics Rule 8.4 (a lawyer shall not engage in conduct involving dishonesty, fraud, deceit, or misrepresentation).

3. When you make that first call, have a copy of your documents with you so you have information on hand to answer their questions. These documents should include the following:

A. A copy of your fee audit
B. A copy of the fee agreement
C. Copies of the disputed invoices

D. Copies of emails and texts relating to the fee dispute
E. Dates/summaries of discussions with your attorney
F. A copy of filed documents that support your claims
G. A record of phone calls to compare with billed time

If you are referred to mediation or arbitration, explain that you believe your attorney may have charged unreasonable fees in violation of ethical rules. Explain that you have documents to support your allegations, and that you would prefer to make a complaint for professional misconduct.

After your initial fact-finding phone call and a review of your state's instructions for filing a complaint (grievance), be prepared to submit a written statement outlining the instances of bill padding and reference your attached audit. Include all supporting documents you have collected to support your overbilling allegations. Your statement should clearly describe what transpired with your attorney and your efforts to resolve the dispute, providing specific dates when possible. Be as detailed and unemotional as possible.

Outlined below is a generic outline intended to provide a basic framework for formatting a complaint. However, it ***is essential to follow the specific instructions provided by your state's bar association.***

My name is___________________________. I am filing a complaint against Attorney _____________________Bar No.________________ for charging unreasonable fees in my case No. ______________.

The following information is provided in support of my complaint:

1. Description of Case: Include the names of the parties involved, the type of case (e.g., family law, civil, probate), the attorneys involved on both sides, and a brief description of the contested issue. Add any additional information that you feel is helpful to describe your situation.

2. Professional Rules of Conduct: Refer to Rule 1.5 and 8.4 of the ABA rules, along with relevant state codes.

3. Timeline of Events and Supporting Documents: Provide a timeline of key events, date case opened, hearings or motions, the length of time the case has been litigated, and any case outcomes if concluded.

4. Fee Agreement: Attach a copy of the agreement, explain how it was provided to you, when and where you signed it, and whether you received any verbal promises before signing.

5. Telephone Log: Describe any discrepancies between billed phone calls and actual call times as noted in your phone log and use your personal phone bill as additional support.

6. Fee Audit: Include a copy of the fee audit you prepared and shared with your attorney, along with their response and any related correspondence about billing questions.

I am requesting the State Bar of ________________ to review this information and determine whether Attorney________________failed to adhere to the Rules of Professional Conduct by charging unreasonable fees. I have attempted to resolve the fee dispute with the attorney (documentation attached), but they failed to respond. I request that an order for restitution be made in the amount of ________________________.

Respectfully submitted,
Client

WHAT HAPPENS AFTER YOU FILE A COMPLAINT?

Every state bar association has its own set of procedural rules, which are usually outlined on the bar's official website. These rules outline the timelines and events that lead up to the outcome of your complaint, which may be handled by the state bar or the state's judiciary. In the best-case scenario, the attorney will adjust their invoice to correct any unreasonable charges. In the worst-case scenario, the bar may determine that the challenged fees, although somewhat excessive, do not rise to the level of an ethics violation.

If the state bar determines that your evidence doesn't support a finding of professional misconduct, you may receive another chance to explain why the fees were unreasonable. You may be able to provide a supplemental explanation that highlights the most obvious examples of bill padding and emphasizes an attorney's obligation as a fiduciary to charge reasonable fees.

If an appeal is not offered, ask for one. Be persistent. If the appeal is unsuccessful, the good news is that you have not yet incurred additional expenses. At this point, however, you will need to decide how much you are willing to invest to formally address your attorney's potentially unethical billing practices.

The available options include: Mediation (a facilitated negotiation process), Arbitration (a potentially binding decision by a neutral third party), and a Civil Lawsuit (a formal court process).

The next chapter explores these alternatives by explaining how each process works and offering insights into the potential advantages and disadvantages of each option.

---

1. *Gurule v. Land Guardian, Inc.*, 912 F3d 252 (5th Cir.2018).
2. American Bar Association, “Preamble and Scope,” Section 12, in *Model Rules of Professional Conduct*, 2020.
3. Levin, Leslie and Robbennolt, Jennifer K., "To Err is Human, To Apologize is Hard: The Role of Apologies in Lawyer Discipline" (2021). *Faculty Articles and Papers. 578.*
4. American Bar Association, “Rule 1.5:Fees,” in *Model Rules of Professional Conduct*, 2020.
5. American Bar Association, “Preamble and Scope,” in *Model Rules of Professional Conduct*, 2020.
6. *Britannica.com* 2025 dictionary. Accessed Feb. 17, 2025.
7. American Bar Association, “Rule 1.5: Fees,” in *Model Rules of Professional Conduct, 2020.*

8. *In re Kutner,* 78 Ill.2d 157, 35 Ill.Dec. 674, 399 N.E.2d 963, 966 (1979) (quoting *The Florida Bar v. Moriber,* 314 So.2d 145, 148 (Fla.1975)).

9. American Bar Association, "Rule 1.5: Fees," in *Model Rules of Professional Conduct,* 2020.

10. Gabriel J. Chin and Scott C. Wells, "Can a Reasonable Doubt Have an Unreasonable Price? Limitations on Attorneys' Fee in Criminal Cases," *Boston College Law Review* 41, no. 1 (December 1, 2000): 1–70.

11. The State Bar of California Standing Committee on Professional Responsibility and Conduct. *Arbitration Advisory no.* 2025-01.

12. *In re Dawson,* 8 P.3d 856, 860 (N.M. 2000).

13. K. William Gibson, ed., *Flying Solo: A Survival Guide for the Solo and Small Firm Lawyer,* 4th ed. (Chicago, Illinois: ABA Law Practice Division, 2014).

14. *Perez v. Kirk Carrigan,* 822 S.W.2d 261, 265 (Tex. App.—Corpus Christi 1991, writ denied).

15. *Committee on Legal Ethics of W. Va. State Bar v. Tatterson,* 352 S.E.2d 107, 113 (W. Va. 1986).

16. *In re Teichner,* 104 Ill. 2d 150, 470 N.E.2d 972 (Ill. 1984).

17. Wisconsin Court System, "Lawyer Regulation," accessed April 2, 2024.

18. Colorado Supreme Court, Office of Attorney Regulation Counsel, "Complaints/Discipline – FAQs, "Accessed April 2, 2024.

19. The State Bar of California, "Complaints & Claims."

20. American Bar Association, "Preamble and Scope." Section 12, in *Model Rules of Professional Conduct,* 2020.

21. The State Bar of California, "Determination of a "Reasonable" Fee," *Arbitration Advisory* 1998-03, 2015.

22. American Bar Association, “Demographics,” in *ABA Profile of the Legal Profession 2023*, 2023.

23. NYSBA Committee on Professional Discipline, “A Guide to Attorney Disciplinary Procedures in New York State,” New York State Bar Association, accessed April 2, 2024

24. “File a Grievance,” State Bar of Texas, accessed April 2, 2024.

25. “Complaints & Claims,” The State Bar of California, accessed April 2, 2024.

26. The State Bar of California, "Analysis of Potential Bill Padding and Other Billing Issues", *Arbitration Advisory* 2016-02, 2015.

27. Weiss, Debra Cassens, “Red-Flag Billing Practices Chronicled; Report Finds ‘upbilling’ by 21 Percent of Law Firms,” *ABA Journal*, March 28, 2017.

28. Weiss, Debra Cassens, “Lawyer Accused of Billing over 24 Hours in a Day Suspended; but Official Said Others Were Worse,” *ABA Journal*, April 26, 2017.

29. www.jud.ct.gov/sgc/faq_public.htm#6

30. www.statebarofsouthdakota.com/lawyer-discipline/

31. https://www.osbar.org/public/legalinfo/1174.htm

32. www.iardc.org/Home/FileComplaint

33. www.floridabar.org/public/acap/assistance

34. https://odc.ohio.gov/fileagrievances

35. www.padisciplinaryboard.org/for-the-public/file-complaint

36. www.wsba.org/docs/default-source/licensing/discipline/2019-10-22-grievance-faq.pdf?sfvrsn=b3103ef1_76

CHAPTER 8
LEGAL ACTION

It may be time........

IMPORTANT NOTE: THIS CHAPTER OFFERS AN EDUCATIONAL OVERVIEW OF THE FORMAL OPTIONS AVAILABLE FOR DISPUTING UNREASONABLE ATTORNEY FEES. CONSULT WITH A QUALIFIED ATTORNEY FOR PERSONALIZED LEGAL GUIDANCE.

"For too many years, lawyer overbilling has been swept under the carpet."[1] And one reason this important topic has not received the attention it deserves is simple: lawyers regulate themselves. The legal profession's system of enforcing its own rules can create perceived conflicts of interest when billing disputes arise.

The process of challenging attorney fees can be complex and intimidating. To address these concerns, this guide focuses on resolving unreasonable fees with the least stressful and most cost-effective methods: an informed discussion with your attorney or, if that fails, filing an ethical complaint with the State Bar.

If discussions with your attorney are unproductive and an ethical complaint does not fully resolve the matter, you may wish to explore more formal options for addressing disputed legal fees. Charging unreasonable fees is unethical in all states; however, the procedures to address such misconduct vary. Your research into available actions should begin with an overview of your state's specific rules and procedures. Chapter 10 provides a comprehensive list of website addresses and phone numbers for state bar associations to help you get started.

ALTERNATIVE DISPUTE RESOLUTION (ADR) vs. CIVIL LAWSUIT

Mediation and arbitration are the most common ADR methods recommended by state bar associations. Although some associations offer these services at no cost, it's still advisable to seek legal advice. There is a potential imbalance of power between an attorney and an unrepresented client, which could lead to an unfair outcome.

Mediation is a non-adversarial process that involves a neutral third party helping you and your attorney reach a voluntary resolution through collaboration and communication. In contrast, arbitration is an adversarial process, with an arbitrator making decisions that can be legally binding or non-binding, depending on the agreement.

Both mediation and arbitration can be less expensive and faster than traditional litigation. They also offer the advantage of maintaining confidentiality if needed.

The disadvantage is that both parties must agree to participate, which can be a significant limitation. You may also overlook a clause in your multi-page fee agreement requiring you to submit all disputes to ADR, unintentionally giving up legal protections that are standard in traditional litigation. Another disadvantage is that discovery is often limited, so important information needed to evaluate your case might not be available.

A **civil lawsuit** can be time-consuming and costly, but it may yield a greater return than using the Alternative Dispute Resolution (ADR) process. However, success rates are relatively low, and stress levels are high. Litigation is expensive because not only would you retain another lawyer and possibly incur court costs, but you will most likely have the added expense of an additional lawyer to serve as an expert witness to support your case. Lawyers have a fiduciary duty to their clients, but ironically, when they breach that duty by intentionally overbilling, clients may end up bearing the financial burden of confronting an attorney's unethical behavior.

MEDIATION

"The challenge of mediation is that the process doesn't work for anybody unless it works for everybody."[2]

Mediation may be your best option if you would like to continue the relationship with your attorney. Mediation is a non-adversarial, informal method of using a neutral third party to help you and your attorney resolve your differences. Since mediation involves compromise, it will not work if you are determined to win at all costs. You are expected to make a good-faith effort to negotiate a settlement rather than wage an all-out war against your attorney.

For mediation to be successful, the parties should use honesty, cooperation, and fairness in their dealings with each other. However, since mediation is so informal, the whole truth is sometimes difficult to uncover. One significant disadvantage of mediation is the potential for an unequal balance of power, especially when attempting mediation without legal representation. Remember, the mediator is neutral, *not* your advocate or your friend.

The mediator and your attorney are both experienced with the mediation process. If you decide to try mediation alone, you risk being persuaded into accepting a settlement that may not be in your best interest. There is also the possibility that you and your attorney may not be able to reach a settlement; thus, time and money could be wasted.

One of the most important features of mediation is confidentiality because it "promotes the free flow of information that may result in the settlement of a dispute."[3] Anything said during mediation stays confidential. Neither party can use admissions made in mediation in subsequent legal proceedings. There are some very narrow exceptions to this rule, but the courts steadfastly protect the confidentiality of mediation.

PROCEDURAL STEPS IN MEDIATION:

1. Mediator Remarks
The mediator describes their role and provides guidelines for the mediation process. It is essential to remember that a mediator is neutral. They do not act as your lawyer.

2. **Opening Statements**
You and your attorney will each have the opportunity to present your respective views. This is where your audit will provide important information about the claim of unreasonable fees. It is essential to assemble all the documents supporting your audit before attending mediation. (See Chapter 7)

3. **Joint Discussion**
After each side has made their opening statement, the mediator will facilitate an exchange of information in a businesslike manner and maintain a civil discussion. You and your attorney will discuss each side of the dispute with the mediator's assistance. Keeping an open mind and listening to your attorney's response will be essential.

4. **Individual Meetings**
The mediator may take each party into a separate room for individual sessions (known as a caucus) to discuss the differences between the parties' positions. During these meetings, the mediator reviews your evidence alongside your attorney's response in an attempt to help both sides reach a resolution. This is where the mediator's neutrality is critical. It is also where power imbalances can emerge, making it important for you to stand your ground.

5. **Negotiation**
After both sides have met privately with the mediator, sometimes with the mediator going back and forth several times between the parties, you will all come together to see if the individual discussions have led you to understand the other side's arguments. If so, you may work out an agreement that is acceptable to both parties.

6. **Settlement**
If you and your attorney have come to a mutual understanding, you can formalize the agreement into an enforceable contract.

I took part in a mediation between two parents at the beginning of their divorce. They each wanted to reach a custody agreement, but both were highly emotional about the issue. The mother alleged domestic abuse, which the father denied. When the session began, he immediately tried to control the conversation, and it became clear that the mother was intimidated. The strain between the two of them, due to numerous issues, made cooperation impossible.

The lesson learned: for mediation to succeed, both parties must approach the process with a willingness to work together with respect, rather than resorting to coercion.

In a mediated fee dispute, an attorney has a clear advantage over a client with no legal experience and no advocate. Nonetheless, some state bar associations divert fee disputes to forums that clients may find unbalanced. If your state's bar association offers mediation at no cost and you are committed to representing yourself, it can be a useful option.

If you approach the process in good faith, with a genuine intent to resolve the dispute, you can gain valuable insight into the strengths and weaknesses of your case.

ARBITRATION

Binding and Nonbinding

There are two types of arbitration: binding and nonbinding. Understanding the difference between them is essential, as your rights and options vary under each process. In binding arbitration, the parties agree to accept the arbitrator's decision as final, which limits their right to seek resolution in court. In contrast, nonbinding arbitration allows either party to reject the arbitrator's decision, providing an option to pursue further litigation if necessary.

PROCEDURAL STEPS IN ARBITRATION:

1. Initiation of the Case
Administrative activities are conducted, including preparing a notice of arbitration, scheduling dates for upcoming steps, providing information regarding the arbitration procedure, and addressing applicable fees.

2. Arbitrator Selection
An arbitrator is appointed, along with information on how to object to the named arbitrator if needed. Procedures for the arbitration process will be outlined.

3. Preliminary Hearing Conference
A preliminary conference is held after the arbitrator's appointment and confirmation. Preliminary issues are addressed, the exchange of information between the parties

is scheduled, and a hearing date is set. The arbitrator will provide a written document confirming all essential dates and specifics discussed.

4. Hearing

The parties present their case to the arbitrator in person, over the telephone, via Zoom, or through the parties submitting written documents. The parties' arbitration agreement and the applicable rules that govern the case will dictate the process.

5. Award

After the hearing is completed and the arbitrator determines that no more evidence will be presented, the hearing(s) are closed, and a date for the issuance of the award is set. The arbitrator presents a written award outlining the outcome of the case and sends it to the parties. At this point, the case is over.

Early in my legal career, I volunteered to act as an arbitrator for the local bar association. Another attorney and I, along with a member of the public, comprised the three-person arbitration panel for a fee dispute. The client and the attorney involved in the dispute were allowed to object to any of the arbitrators. No objections were made. The client was a young man having issues with his family lawyer's fees. The non-lawyer and I agreed that many of the attorney's charges were excessive for several reasons. The other attorney disagreed, but fees were reduced because of the 2-to-1 vote of the arbitration panel.

Subsequently, I was asked to serve on another arbitration panel. This time, the case involved a fee dispute with the same attorney who had previously voted against reducing fees. The attorney, now involved in their own fee dispute, objected to my participation and assignment to their case.

The above narrative is an example of how experienced attorneys can gain a significant advantage over less knowledgeable clients. Attorneys may leverage information unknown to clients or utilize negotiation skills to resolve disputes in their favor. Given that *binding* arbitration typically precludes appeals, this underscores the importance of legal assistance and the additional expenses that may result.

Note that your fee agreement may require you to resolve all disputes through arbitration. Some attorneys include clauses stating that both fee disputes and malpractice claims must be handled through binding arbitration. This is another reason to carefully review your fee agreement and fully understand its terms before signing.

One county bar association advocated for the inclusion of binding arbitration clauses in fee agreements. While the association emphasized the importance of a smooth execution of a fee agreement, it did not find it necessary to require lawyers to explain arbitration terms in detail. This approach raises the question of whether expediency takes precedence over a client's understanding of the agreement's terms.

Arbitration can be a useful and cost-effective alternative to litigation, as long as you understand the rights you may be giving up. Because arbitration may involve procedural rules that require specialized legal knowledge, it is important to familiarize yourself with the process. Contact your state's fee arbitration program for more information.

CIVIL LAWSUIT

"Avoid lawsuits beyond all things; they pervert your conscience, impair your health, and dissipate your property." [4]

I was 48 when I graduated from law school shortly after my divorce. During that time, I observed numerous instances of unprofessional conduct by attorneys both inside and outside the courtroom. Upon entering legal practice, I decided to help family law litigants avoid similar difficulties. Because I believe that lawyers should be held accountable for unethical behavior, a problem I witnessed too often, I represented clients in legal malpractice cases alongside family law matters.

A legal malpractice lawsuit may arise when an attorney breaches a duty owed to a client during representation. By its nature, litigation is adversarial and can be an uphill battle. Pursuing a malpractice claim typically requires hiring a second attorney and an expert witness to testify that your former attorney did not meet the required standard of care. Many malpractice attorneys handle cases on a contingency-fee basis if the case meets their selection criteria. Others bill the client by the hour, and clients are also responsible for court costs and related litigation expenses.

The four basic elements of a legal malpractice case are: duty, breach, causation and damages.

Duty

A landmark case[5] explained an attorney's duty: "The general rule with respect to the liability of an attorney for failure to properly perform his duties to his client is that the attorney, by accepting employment to give legal advice or to render other legal services, impliedly agrees to use such skill, prudence, and diligence as lawyers of ordinary skill and capacity commonly possess and exercise in the performance of the tasks which they undertake."

Breach

A breach occurs when an attorney violates a client's trust by failing to meet the expected standard of care and acting in their own interest rather than in the best interests of the client.

Causation

To establish causation, the client must show that the attorney's conduct directly caused the client harm, but this can be very difficult to prove. A client must demonstrate that a better outcome would likely have occurred but for the attorney's misconduct. According to one legal scholar, citing an ABA study, only a small percentage of legal malpractice cases that go to trial result in a favorable ruling for the plaintiff.[6]

Damages

A client must prove they suffered measurable financial harm directly caused by the attorney's negligence.

Legal malpractice is defined by law. "An action for legal malpractice requires proof that the attorney failed to exercise the reasonable skill and knowledge ordinarily possessed by a member of the legal profession, that this negligence was the proximate cause of the client's loss or injury, and that the client sustained actual damages."[7]

When an attorney intentionally charges unreasonable fees, it is a breach of their fiduciary duty and a violation of their professional rules of conduct. While this behavior may cause financial harm, surprisingly it does not always meet the requirements for a malpractice claim. Recognizing this distinction can help clients pursue the appropriate remedy, whether through mediation, fee arbitration, or litigation. In addition to legal malpractice, other causes of action against attorneys include breach of fiduciary duty, breach of contract, infliction of emotional distress, and fraud.

The greatest disadvantage to a lawsuit is the high cost of pursuing a claim. Already financially strained from excessive legal bills, many clients simply lack the resources to pursue litigation. However, a legal malpractice action may offer the recovery of damages beyond the reimbursement of excessive fees.

If you are considering legal action against your attorney for unreasonable fees, it is crucial to obtain legal advice to fully understand your options before pursuing your claim.

WHAT IS THE DIFFERENCE BETWEEN PROFESSIONAL MISCONDUCT AND LEGAL MALPRACTICE?

The key difference between a professional misconduct complaint and a legal malpractice lawsuit is the stated objective. Disciplinary proceedings aim to to protect the public and maintain professional standards. A civil lawsuit seeks to recover damages for the harm caused by an attorney's negligence. And herein lies the problem. A State Bar may discipline an attorney for charging unreasonable fees, but decline to order restitution. As a result the existing self-regulatory disciplinary framework can impede a client's ability to obtain financial accountability for an attorney's misconduct.

A client is often forced to pursue additional, separate fee-dispute proceedings to obtain reimbursement for excessive fees. The good news is that a disciplinary finding against an attorney for unreasonable fees can strongly support the client's position in subsequent proceedings.

For a more detailed analysis of an attorney's professionalism in relation to legal malpractice, consider a law professor's article titled "The Intersection of Legal Malpractice and Professionalism."[8] While this topic extends well beyond the scope of this book, whether you are an considering an attorney's professional misconduct or alleged legal malpractice, it is essential to remember: [T]he foundation of an attorney's relationship with clients and the legal system is trust."[9] And a breach of that trust is unjustifiable.

SUMMARY: WHAT ARE YOUR OPTIONS: MEDIATION? ARBITRATION? LAWSUIT?

It is essential to consider two fundamental factors: the emotional stress and the financial cost of legal actions.

Initiating a formal proceeding against an attorney can be stressful and costly. Mediation is typically the least adversarial option, but may still pose challenges to those unfamiliar with the process. Arbitration generally incurs lower costs than litigation, but understanding the difference between non-binding and binding arbitration is crucial. Pursuing a civil lawsuit may offer a greater potential recovery, but it is often the most expensive option and has a lower success rate.

Addressing unethical fees should not be so difficult for clients who hired an attorney to protect their rights in the first place. While your attorney is obligated to charge reasonable fees, you must still be prepared to assert your right to fair and ethical billing.

Section 9 of the Preamble to the ABA Model Rules[10] acknowledges that attorneys may face ethical conflicts between their duty to clients and the practical need to earn a "satisfactory living." But remember, an attorney is also a fiduciary, and as one commentator has observed, "[s]tealing is bad enough, but when one's trusted counselor is the culprit, it is indefensible."[11]

Section 19 of the Preamble states that a failure to comply with a rule is a basis for "invoking the disciplinary process."[12] Yet it seems that state bar associations, tasked with administering the disciplinary process, often shift the burden onto the client to resolve conflicts of unreasonable fees by forcing them into formal proceedings caused by an attorney's violation of their ethical duties.

Important note: There is a better alternative to costly litigation. State bar associations must confront an uncomfortable truth: the current disciplinary system is often perceived as protecting attorneys at the expense of the public. When disputes over unreasonable fees are dismissed as mere contractual disagreements, the message to clients is clear—ethical rules may be applied selectively.

Documented evidence of an attorney's intentional overbilling should be handled as a professional misconduct complaint. Every state bar should provide a transparent and accessible procedure for clients to obtain restitution when fees are proven to be unreasonable. If state bar associations would only recognize the serious harm caused by unethical billing, they could strengthen public trust in a profession that depends on it.

Unreasonable legal fees force clients into a difficult position: either pay the excessive charges or pay the costs of challenging them. Meaningful enforcement of ethical rules along with financial accountability could prevent this problem. Otherwise, the experience can feel less like legal representation and more like an Attorney Fee Hu$tle.

1. Darlene Ricker, "Greed, Ignorance, and Overbilling: Some Lawyers Have Given New Meaning to the Term 'Legal Fiction,'" *ABA Journal 80*, no. 8 (1994): 62–66).

2. "Preparing for a Mediation," United States Court of Appeals for the Fourth Circuit, accessed February 1, 2025. Disclaimer: The permitted use of this quotation does not constitute an endorsement of the book or its contents by the judiciary or this court.

3. *In re Teligent, Inc.*, 640 F.3d 53, 57-58 (2d Cir. 2011).

4. Jean de la Bruyere, 17th century French philosopher.

5. *Lucas V. Hamm*, 56 Cal.2 583, (CA Supreme Court 1961).

6. Ramos, Manual, "Legal Malpractice: The Profession's Dirty Little Secret," *Vanderbilt Law Review* 47, no. 6 (1994): 1657.

7. *Kreamer v. Town of Oxford*, 96 A.D.3d 1128, 946 N.Y.S.2d 283, 2012 N.Y. Slip Op. 4445 (N.Y. App. Div. 2012).

8. Boothe-Perry, Nicola A. "No Laughing Matter: The Intersection of Legal Malpractice and Professionalism." American University Journal of Gender Social Policy and Law 21, no. 1 (2012): 1-37.

9. *Mattson*, 2002 S.D. 112, ¶ 55, 651 N.W.2d at 289 (quoting *In re Discipline of Tidball*, 503 N.W.2d 850, 856 (S.D. 1993)).

10. American Bar Association, "Preamble and Scope," in *Model Rules of Professional Conduct*, 2020.

11. Schachner, Robert W. and Phillips, John, *How & When to Sue Your Lawyer: What You Need to Know* (Garden City Park, N.Y: Square One Publishers, 2005).

12. American Bar Association, "Preamble and Scope," in *Model Rules of Professional Conduct*, 2020.

CHAPTER 9
TOOL KIT

Checklists, templates, resources, and websites

This chapter compiles checklists and templates from the book for your convenience. Additional resources are available at www.attorneyfeehustle.com, where you can submit questions, participate in the Q&A forum, and access regularly updated information to help you dispute unreasonable attorney fees. Scan the QR code for direct access to the website.

TEN TIPS TO PROTECT YOURSELF AGAINST EXCESSIVE LEGAL FEES

1. Choose your attorney wisely
2. Collect your documents
3. Read and question the fee agreement
4. Do not sign the fee agreement in the office
5. Think twice before calling your attorney
6. Start a telephone log
7. Promptly review each invoice
8. Identify and document potential bill-padding
9. Communicate with your attorney
10. Challenge excessive attorney fees

UNBUNDLING LEGAL SERVICES

Unbundling legal services, or limited-scope representation, allows an attorney to handle only a portion of the tasks required for a legal matter. For example, the attorney would review a contract, draft a motion, or prepare the client for an upcoming hearing, leaving the client responsible for the remaining aspects of the case. The legal service could be billed by the hour or on a fixed fee basis. This approach can reduce legal costs and give clients more control, but it also requires a detailed written agreement to prevent any confusion about the attorney's responsibilities. The American Bar Association provides an unbundling resource center website that lists the rules for every state. www.americanbar.org/groups/delivery_legal_services/resources/pro_se_unbundling_resource_center/court_rules/

FEE AGREEMENT CHECKLIST

Use this checklist to review your attorney's fee agreement before signing. A written agreement protects both you and your attorney, reduces misunderstandings, and helps prevent unreasonable fees.

General Requirements

-Do I have a written fee agreement?
-Is the scope of representation clearly stated?
-Does the agreement specify the amount of retainer?
-Is there an explanation for termination?
-Have I received a copy signed by both parties?

Retainers

-Is the type of retainer clearly explained?
-For deposits: Will unused funds be returned to me?
-Will the retainer be placed in a client trust account?
-What happens when my original retainer is exhausted?
-Can the attorney withdraw funds without prior notice?

Billing Method

-Is the billing method identified?
-For hourly billing: Are attorney and staff rates listed?
-Are billing increments specified?
-For flat fee: Is the exact scope of work described in writing?
-For contingency: Is the percentage fee stated?
-Are potential expenses outlined?
-Can billing rates increase during the representation?
-How frequently will I receive itemized invoices?
-Am I charged for administrative or clerical tasks?
-Are interest charges or late fees disclosed?

Key Terms to Review

-Does the agreement contain an arbitration clause?

-Is the arbitration binding or non-binding ?

-Is there a deadline to dispute charges on invoices?

-Do I understand the type of lien, if any?

Final Step

-Have I asked for an explanation of terms I don't understand?

-Do I fully comprehend my financial obligations?

18 POTENTIAL BILL PADDING PRACTICES

1. **A lack of detail in describing an attorney's charges**
2. **A lack of detail in describing staff charges**
3. **Billing expenses above cost**
4. **Billing for tasks not performed**
5. **Block billing**
6. **Charges for clerical tasks billed by a paralegal**
7. **Charges for paralegal tasks billed by an attorney**
8. **Charges related to billing questions**
9. **Chipping**
10. **Churning**
11. **Duplicate billing**
12. **Excessive entries for document review**
13. **Excessive legal research**
14. **Excessive time to complete a task**
15. **Fees not in compliance with the fee agreement**
16. **High minimum increments**
17. **The overuse of "rounded" time estimates**
18. **Vague descriptions**

EXAMPLES OF VAGUE DESCRIPTIONS

Ask yourself, "Can I determine from the description what work was completed and why it was necessary?" If the answer is no, flag the entry and request clarification.

Case analysis
Case development
Communicate with
Conference
Draft document
Draft pleadings
Email
Fact investigation
Filing
Further work on matter
Hearing preparation
Legal research
Meeting
Phone call
Prepare for conference
Prepare for discovery
Prepare for hearing/motion
Prepare for trial
Research
Review documents
Review materials
Review records
Strategy session
Work on brief
Work on case

EXAMPLES OF SUBSTANTIVE LEGAL WORK PROVIDED BY PARALEGALS

Work that would have been performed by an attorney
Contacting state agencies
Legal research
Factual investigations
Assisting with depositions and discovery
Compiling statistical and financial data
Legal citation checking
Correspondence with clients, counsel, courts
Drafting or reviewing legal documents[1]

EXAMPLES OF POTENTIALLY NON-BILLABLE CLERICAL TASKS

calendaring
converting files to PDF
copying documents
faxing
filing
formatting
mailing letters
making bank deposits
organizing file folders
scanning
scheduling
uploading documents

OPTIONS TO DISPUTE UNREASONABLE ATTORNEY FEES

Discussion with your attorney – Begin your dispute with a respectful yet detailed conversation about specific charges. Provide a copy of your audit to the attorney for review.

File a complaint with the state bar – If your attorney refuses to provide a reasonable explanation or fails to adjust excessive fees, you can independently file a professional misconduct complaint. State bar associations investigate ethical violations at no cost, but you may need to be persistent and specifically request restitution.

Request mediation or arbitration – Many state bars and courts offer low-cost or no-cost fee dispute programs. Mediation or arbitration provides a neutral forum to resolve billing disputes without the expense of a lawsuit. However, to protect your rights, expenses for advocacy may be required if you are unfamiliar with mediation or arbitration proceedings.

File a lawsuit (as a last resort) – Litigation should only be pursued if all other options fail. While it can provide the greatest return, it is stressful, costly, and time-consuming.

LEGAL FEE AUDIT CHECKLIST

1. Examine the invoice immediately upon receipt
2. Check dispute deadlines in fee agreement
3. Verify hourly rates for each staff member
4. Review billing increment policy
5. Check expense policy
6. Compare charges to fee agreement
7. Identify excessive charges. See Chapters 4 and 5.
8. For each disputed entry notate:
   A. Date
   B. Task description (verbatim)
   C. Time billed
   D. Staff name and rate
   E. Total disputed fee
   F. Reason for dispute (refer to 18 bill padding practices list)
9. Compile information into audit template
10. Send a copy to attorney for justification of charges

An audit provides a clear, organized record of the charges you are questioning and the specific reasons for each disputed entry.

When you include the date, task description, the person who performed the work, the rate charged, and your explanation for concern, you create an itemized report that is difficult to ignore. This approach not only keeps the discussion focused on the facts but also shifts the burden to the attorney to justify each charge. A well-prepared audit also shows that you are organized, informed and prepared to hold your attorney accountable for questionable billing practices.

AUDIT TEMPLATE

INVOICE ANALYSIS: *Client*		INV. # *1234*				INV. DATE: *6/1/24*	ABC LAW FIRM
DATE	DESCRIPTION of LEGAL SERVICE	ATTY HRS	RATE	STAFF HRS	RATE	AMOUNT	REASON for DISPUTE

SAMPLE LETTER TO YOUR ATTORNEY

Dear Attorney,

As a follow-up to our recent discussion regarding Invoice #1234, dated May 1, 2025, I would like to provide additional information for your review. I've attached a spreadsheet identifying the specific charges we discussed, along with a brief explanation of my concerns.

For example, several clerical tasks billed on April 16 appear similar to entries billed on April 2. In addition, three entries dated April 8, 9, and 10 contain descriptions that are too vague for me to fully understand the legal work performed. I've also included several entries that are a bit confusing, and it would help if you could explain if and when these documents were filed.

Thank you. I appreciate your time and assistance in addressing these billing questions.

Sincerely,
Client

HOW TO FILE A COMPLAINT FOR PROFESSIONAL MISCONDUCT DUE TO UNREASONABLE FEES

Start with a fact-finding call to your state bar. (Chapter 10)

Explain that you have identified and documented problematic fees on your invoice that you believe may violate ABA Rule 1.5 (unreasonable fees) and Rule 8.4 regarding billing practices. Describe your efforts to discuss the matter with your attorney and the results of those discussions.

Have the following documents available:

Fee audit
The retainer agreement
Copies of disputed invoices
Emails and texts regarding fees
Notes from conversations with your attorney
Proof (or lack) of work products billed
A call log (actual time vs. billed time)

Inform the State Bar that you are requesting restitution if the fees are found to be unreasonable. Ask about the options that your State has for disputing fees because of your attorney's alleged misconduct. You may be directed to file an official complaint. An example is provided on the next page.

OUTLINE OF A STATE BAR COMPLAINT

Outlined below is a generic outline intended to provide a basic framework for formatting a complaint. However, it ***is essential to follow the specific instructions provided by your state's bar association.***

My name is________________________. I am filing a complaint against Attorney __________________
Bar No.______________ for charging unreasonable fees in my case No. _____________.

The following information is provided in support of my complaint:

1. Description of Case: Include the names of the parties involved, the type of case (e.g., family law, civil, probate), the attorneys involved on both sides, and a brief description of the contested issue. Add any additional information that you may feel is helpful to describe your concerns.

2. Professional Rules of Conduct: Refer to Rule 1.5 and 8.4 of the ABA rules, along with relevant state codes.

3. Timeline of Events and Supporting Documents: Provide a timeline of key events, date case opened, hearings or motions, the length of time the case has been litigated, and any case outcomes if concluded.

4. Fee Agreement: Attach a copy of the agreement, explain how it was provided to you, when and where you signed it, and whether you received any verbal promises before signing.

5. Telephone Log: Describe any discrepancies between billed phone calls and actual call times, using your personal phone bill.

6. Fee Audit: Include a copy of the fee audit you prepared and shared with your attorney, along with their response and any related correspondence about billing questions.

I respectfully request the State Bar of ________________ to review this information and determine whether Attorney________________failed to adhere to the Rules of Professional Conduct by charging unreasonable fees. I have attempted to resolve the fee issues with the attorney (documentation attached), but they failed to respond. I request that an order for restitution be made in the amount of ________________________.

Respectfully submitted,
Client

BASIC ELEMENTS OF A LEGAL MALPRACTICE CASE

Duty

A landmark case[2] explained an attorney's duty: "The general rule with respect to the liability of an attorney for failure to properly perform his duties to his client is that the attorney, by accepting employment to give legal advice or to render other legal services, impliedly agrees to use such skill, prudence, and diligence as lawyers of ordinary skill and capacity commonly possess and exercise in the performance of the tasks which they undertake."

Breach

A breach occurs when an attorney violates a client's trust by failing to meet the expected standard of care and acting in their own interest rather than in the best interests of the client.

Causation

To establish causation, the client must show that the attorney's conduct directly caused the client harm, but this can be very difficult to prove. A client must demonstrate that a better outcome would likely have occurred but for the attorney's misconduct. According to one legal scholar, citing an ABA study, only a small percentage of legal malpractice cases that go to trial result in a favorable ruling for the plaintiff.[3]

Damages

A client must prove they suffered measurable financial harm directly caused by the attorney's negligence.

FREE ONLINE RESOURCES

American Arbitration Association Consumer Arbitration Rules
https://www.adr.org/industries/consumer/#rules-forms-and-fees

American Bar Association Model Rules of Professional Conduct:
https://www.americanbar.org/groups/professional_responsibility/publications/model_rules_of_professional_conduct/model_rules_of_professional_conduct_table_of_contents/

American Bar Association Formal Opinion 93-379 December 6, 1993 Billing for Professional Fees, Disbursements and Other Expenses
https://nvbar.org/wp-content/uploads/ABA_Formal_Opinion_93-379.pd

American Bar Association Suggested resources if you have problems with your lawyer
https://www.americanbar.org/groups/legal_services/flh-home/flh-trouble-with-a-lawyer/

AVVO
https://www.avvo.com/

COURT LISTENER
https://www.courtlistener.com/

FINDLAW
https://www.findlaw.com/

GOOGLE SCHOLAR
https://scholar.google.com/schhp?hl=en&num=1&as_sdt=2003

JUSTIA
https://law.justia.com/

LAWHELP.org
https://www.lawhelp.org/

LIBRARY OF CONGRESS
https://guides.loc.gov/

---

1. McMackin v. McMackin, 651 A.2d 778 (Del. Fam. 1993).
2. *Lucas V. Hamm,* 56 Cal.2 583, (CA Supreme Court 1961).
3. Ramos, Manual, "Legal Malpractice: The Profession's Dirty Little Secret," *Vanderbilt Law Review* 47, no. 6 (1994): 1657.

CHAPTER 10

STATE BAR ASSOCIATIONS

The public's friend or foe?

The American Bar Association's Model Rules of Professional Conduct, specifically Section 1.5, prohibit attorneys from charging or collecting unreasonable fees. This rule, in some form, has been adopted by all 50 states. Perhaps it's time to encourage the legal profession to seriously address the issue of intentional overbilling, as the profession, after all, is largely self-regulating. Currently, disputing unethical fees can be a complicated and costly process. As a result, it is often difficult to have an unreasonable fee dispute treated as a disciplinary matter. To uphold the profession's ethical standards, state bar associations should take a more proactive role in investigating complaints of unreasonable fees. While attorneys are entitled to bill for every minute genuinely spent on a case, billing for work not performed is unethical and indefensible.

STATE BAR ASSOCIATIONS

Note: The following links and phone numbers are current as of the publication date, but subsequent website changes might invalidate the information provided. Phone numbers are included as many state bar associations initially recommend calling for information before initiating a fee dispute.

ALABAMA: Alabama State Bar
334-269-1515
https://www.alabar.org/assets/2025/04/Complaint-form_brochure-2012.pdf

ALASKA: Alaska Bar Association
907-272-7469
https://alaskabar.org/ethics-discipline

ARIZONA: State Bar of Arizona
602-340-7280
https://www.azbar.org/for-the-public/concerns-about-your-legal-professional/submitting-a-cha

ARKANSAS: Arkansas Bar Association
501-376-0313
https://www.arcourts.gov/professional-conduct

CALIFORNIA: The State Bar of California
415-538-2000
https://www.calbar.ca.gov/Public/Complaints-Claims

COLORADO: Colorado Bar Association
303-860-1115
https://www.cobar.org/For-the-Public

CONNECTICUT: Connecticut Bar Association
860-223-4400
https://www.ctbar.org/public

DELAWARE: Delaware State Bar Association
302-658-5279
https://www.dsba.org/sections-committees/standing-committees/fee-dispute/

DISTRICT OF COLUMBIA: District of Columbia
202-737-4700
https://www.dcbar.org/Attorney-Discipline/For-the-Public

FLORIDA: The Florida Bar
850-561-5600
https://floridabar.org/public/acap/

GEORGIA: State Bar of Georgia
404-527-8700
https://www.gabar.org/public/file-a-complaint

HAWAII: Hawaii State Bar Association
808-537-1868
https://dbhawaii.org/the-attorney-disciplinary-complaint-process/

IDAHO: Idaho State Bar
208-334-4500
https://isb.idaho.gov/bar-counsel/grievance-faq/

ILLINOIS: Illinois State Bar Association
312-565-2600
http://www.iardc.org/Home/FileComplain

INDIANA: Indiana State Bar Association

317- 232-1807

https://www.in.gov/courts/ojar/di-process/complaint/

IOWA: Iowa State Bar Association

515-243-3179

https://www.iowacourts.gov/opr/attorneys/attorney-discipline/complaint-against-a-lawyer

KANSAS: Kansas Bar Association

785-234-5696

https://www.kscourts.gov/Attorneys/Office-of-Disciplinary-Administration/File-a-Complaint

KENTUCKY: Kentucky Bar Association

502-564-3795

https://kybar.org/For-Public

LOUISIANA: Louisiana State Bar Association

504-566-1600

https://www.lsba.org/Public/AttorneyDisciplinaryProcedures.aspx

MAINE: Maine State Bar Association

207-623-1121

https://mebaroverseers.org/complaint/index.html

MARYLAND: Maryland State Bar Association

410-685-7878

https://www.courts.state.md.us/attygrievance/complaint

MASSACHUSETTS: Massachusetts Bar Association
617-338-0500
https://www.massbbo.org/s/complaints

MICHIGAN: State Bar of Michigan
517-346-6300
https://www.agcmi.org/for-the-public/investigation

MINNESOTA: Minnesota State Bar Association
612-333-1183
http://lprb.mncourts.gov/complaints/Pages/default.aspx

MISSISSIPPI: The Mississippi Bar
601-948-4471
https://www.msbar.org/ethics-discipline/

MISSOURI: The Missouri Bar
573-635-4128
http://missourilawyershelp.org/public-resources/

MONTANA: State Bar of Montana
406-442-7660
https://courts.mt.gov/forms/AttorneyComplaints

NEBRASKA: Nebraska State Bar Association
402-475-7091
https://nebraskajudicial.gov/administration/professional-ethics/attorney-discipline-ethics/file

NEVADA: State Bar of Nevada
702.382.2200
https://nvbar.org/for-the-public/attorney-discipline

NEW HAMPSHIRE: New Hampshire Bar Association
603-224-6942
https://www.nhbar.org/dispute-with-an-attorney/

NEW JERSEY: New Jersey State Bar Association
732-249-5000
https://www.njcourts.gov/attorneys/attorney-ethics-and-discipline

NEW MEXICO: State Bar of New Mexico
505-797-6000
https://nmdisboard.org/for-the-public/file-a-complaint/

NEW YORK: New York State Bar Association
518-463-3200
https://nysba.org/public-resources/guide-to-attorney-discipline/

NORTH CAROLINA: North Carolina State Bar
919-828-4620
https://www.ncbar.gov/for-the-public/i-am-having-a-dispute-with-a-lawyer/

NORTH DAKOTA: State Bar Assoc. of North Dakota
701-255-1404
https://www.sband.org/page/file_a_complaint

OHIO: Ohio State Bar Association
614-487-2050
https://www.ohiobar.org/public-resources/about-attorneys/lawyer-ethics--discipline/

OKLAHOMA: Oklahoma Bar Association
405-416-7000
https://www.okbar.org/gc/complaint/

OREGON:
503-620-0222
https://www.osbar.org/public/legalinfo/1174.htm

PENNSYLVANIA: Pennsylvania Bar Association
800-932-0311
https://www.padisciplinaryboard.org/for-the-public/file-complaint

RHODE ISLAND: Rhode Island Bar Association
401-421-5740
https://www.courts.ri.gov/programs-services/Pages/disciplinary-board-faqs.aspx

SOUTH CAROLINA: South Carolina Bar
803-799-6653
https://www.scbar.org/public/get-legal-help/problems-your-lawyer/

SOUTH DAKOTA: State Bar of South Dakota
605-224-7554
https://www.statebarofsouthdakota.com/lawyer-discipline

TENNESSEE: Tennessee Bar Association
615-383-7421
https://www.tba.org/?pg=unhappy-with-your-attorney

TEXAS: State Bar of Texas
800-932-1900
https://www.texasbar.com/AM/
Template.cfm?Section=Public_Home

UTAH: Utah State Bar
801-531-9077
https://www.opcutah.org/

VERMONT: Vermont Bar Association
802-223-1400
https://www.vermontjudiciary.org/sites/default/
files/documents/
Brochure%20-%204.1.21%20Revision.pdf

VIRGINIA: Virginia State Bar
804-775-0500
https://www.vsb.org/Site/Site/legal-help/complaints-
claims.aspx
?hkey=3e73485f-8fc2-4b96-91be-db0be05e7bd9

WASHINGTON: Washington State Bar Association
206-443-9722
https://www.wsba.org/for-the-public/concerns-about-a-la
wyer

WEST VIRGINIA: West Virginia State Bar
304-553-7220
https://wvbar.org/public-information/public-programs/

WISCONSIN: State Bar of **Wisconsin**
608-257-3838
https://www.wisbar.org/forPublic/IHaveaDispute
WithMyLawyer
/Pages/i-have-a-dispute-with-my-lawyer.aspx

WYOMING: Wyoming State Bar
307-632-9061
https://www.wyomingbar.org/for-the-public/attorney-com
plaints/

CHAPTER 11

SOMETIMES THE LEGAL SYSTEM DOESN'T WORK

For justice to exist, everyone should have equal access to the courts.

At the 1941 meeting of the American Bar Association, U.S. Supreme Court Justice Wiley Rutledge observed: "Equality before the law in a true democracy is a matter of right. It cannot be a matter of charity or of favor or of grace or of discretion."[1]

Everyone should have access to the legal system, and that includes an ability to correct an injustice: "The public legitimacy of our justice system relies on procedures that are 'neutral, accurate, consistent, trustworthy, and fair,' and that 'provide opportunities for error corrections."[2]

Justice often favors those who can afford competent legal counsel, leaving individuals with limited resources struggling to address perceived errors. As a result, our respected judicial system does not always function as intended—even for legal professionals. The issue of unreasonable attorney fees is deeply personal to me, and sharing my experience is central to why this book was written. My own challenges obtaining adequate representation led me to a better understanding of how excessive attorney fees can prevent a client from effectively participating in their own case.

Without substantial resources, access to justice can be severely limited. I became a lawyer not only to navigate my own divorce, but also to advocate for individuals who found themselves voiceless in family court because of financial constraints. Ultimately, I failed, not because of a lack of commitment, but because I did not have the "money or political clout"[3] to defend against, ironically, an attorney fee complaint. If you read no further than these opening paragraphs, please remember:

Attorneys have an ethical obligation to charge reasonable fees and expenses.[4]

Attorneys bear the burden of proving the reasonableness of the fees they charge.[5]

Attorneys who allow substantial unpaid fee balances to accumulate based on verbal assurances expose themselves to serious professional risk.

As an attorney, I was disbarred after failing to recognize the critical importance of detailed billing practices. My intent was never to overcharge clients. To the contrary, I routinely underbilled to compensate for my lack of attention to invoicing. I focused on my client outcomes, kept my hourly rate low, and billed for less time than I actually worked.

Many of my clients had limited financial resources and had already exhausted their savings due to prior legal expenses. In one custody case, a client's former spouse complained to the court that the fees I charged were substantially lower than those charged by her own attorney, and that she felt disadvantaged as a result.

I represented my clients conscientiously and respectfully. I acknowledge that I made invoicing errors and take responsibility for them. Unfortunately, a reliance on verbal assurances and informal billing practices ultimately resulted in my disbarment and incarceration.

I naively assumed that underbilling would protect both my clients and my practice. I believed that if my fees were ever questioned, my policy of undercharging would address any concerns about excessive fees. However, that strategy turned out to be a big mistake.

The devastating outcome of my experience demonstrates the critical importance of transparent billing practices that protect both clients and attorneys. This guide is intended to help clients dispute potentially unreasonable fees, but it can also serve as reminder to solo practitioners about the absolute necessity of providing clear and detailed invoices.

A personal note: *While I certainly disagree with the outcome of my case, I have chosen not to revisit specific details out of respect for those involved. Instead, my goal is to focus on the lessons I learned as an attorney, educator, and litigant. This guide looks at the bigger picture: how unethical billing practices and high attorney fees can stand in the way of a fair outcome.*

I've added a personal account that reflects the central theme of this book. Whether you are unable to hire counsel at the start or become overwhelmed by unreasonable fees in the middle of your case, the result is the same: justice becomes elusive. Access to justice should never depend on the size of your bank account. Attorneys are not merely business professionals; they carry a "special responsibility for the quality of justice."[6]

My ill-fated journey began with a California State Bar hearing.

STATE BAR HEARING

State Bar Associations tend to focus on sole practitioners more often than attorneys in large firms. A legal professor noted that, according to a California State Bar survey, 78% of disciplinary cases prosecuted and completed involved solo practitioners, even though they represented only 23% of the lawyers practicing in that state.[7] An Oregon State Bar survey revealed that solo practitioners received 80% of their disciplinary sanctions.[8]

These disciplinary statistics indicate that the sanctioned attorneys are often from small offices and lack the institutional resources available to larger firms. As a sole practitioner representing myself, I was particularly vulnerable to the disciplinary process. Earlier in this book, I discussed examples of large law firms overbilling and having their requested fees reduced by audits or court rulings. Yet disciplinary action in such cases is relatively infrequent.

One example: It took **205 client complaints and nearly 40 years** before a State Bar publicly disciplined Thomas Girardi of Girardi & Keese.[9] An independent investigation initiated by the California State Bar "determined that Girardi cultivated contacts on the Board, in the Executive Director's Office, and in the Office of Chief Trial Counsel ("OCTC"), both at the managerial and line prosecutor and investigator level." Despite disciplinary matters "involving allegations of trust accounting violations, theft, perjury, and other serious infractions,"[10] Mr. Girardi was not disbarred until 2022, despite disciplinary complaints against him dating back to 1984.

I did not have the funds to retain counsel specializing in State Bar defense. One of the state bar defense lawyers I consulted was so expensive that I knew I could never afford the fees. He told me that he carried a personal credit card machine (not a common sight 14 years ago) to collect payments on the spot. Faced with limited options, I decided to defend myself. Looking back, that was a big mistake.

I became an example of the age-old warning: "The lawyer who represents himself has a fool for a client." As I had no experience in disciplinary or criminal proceedings, I was unprepared to deal with numerous legal matters that arose before, during, and after the hearing. Significant Fifth Amendment issues arose, and in my view, the process raised serious due-process questions. I believe procedural protections were sacrificed for convenience.

I respect our legal system. Its complex structure, composed of laws, codes, regulations, and statutes, serves as a constitutional safeguard for everyday citizens.

Unfortunately, I believe the State Bar, whose mission is the "...support of efforts for greater access to, and inclusion in, the legal system..."[11] failed to provide me with a fair hearing because they neglected to adequately address the direct impact of disciplinary findings on my liberty interests.

I was informed personally by the state bar prosecutor that I was not entitled to appointed counsel for the hearing. Although appointed counsel is not typically provided in disciplinary hearings, there is an exception. Because I believe that the State Bar was well aware of potential criminal proceedings, that knowledge supports an argument for appointing counsel. In my case, there was a "possible deprivation of my liberty"[12] if the State Bar did not rule in my favor, which is precisely what happened.

The results of the State Bar hearing were used in the subsequent criminal case, but proceedings involving both disciplinary hearings and criminal charges are somewhat complex. Not only does the ABA suggest deferring disciplinary proceedings until the conclusion of criminal litigation involving similar allegations, but its rules for lawyer disciplinary enforcement offer an option for appointed counsel "upon such terms and subject to such provisions as justice and equity may require."[13]

The ABA safeguards were not applied in my case. I believe the prosecutor's actions raised serious concerns about my right to a fair trial. Criminal charges were not filed until *after* the State Bar's hearing. I believe not only were there significant due process issues but also a critical question: if the allegations were so egregious, why weren't criminal charges filed first?

A year later, after the hearing, I discovered a California State Bar case[14] that denied an attorney's request for appointed counsel. The Court stated, "Obviously, petitioner here is not in any sense put at risk as regards his physical liberty by the disciplinary proceedings against him and consequently cannot demonstrate a right to assistance of counsel." Because that very risk did exist in my case, I believe my constitutional protections were simply ignored.

The State Bar's initial decision was not in my favor. I felt the issues I faced at trial would not have developed if I had been represented by experienced counsel. For example, a jointly retained handwriting expert confirmed a signature on a fee agreement, but the court appeared to overlook that information. At the review hearing, I believe the prosecutor presented an inaccurate statement regarding declarations signed under penalty of perjury. It just seemed to me that the State Bar gave limited consideration to my *pro se* arguments throughout the proceedings.

I later discovered that during the same period, the State Bar ignored numerous disciplinary cases involving the previously mentioned, politically connected attorney. The 2023 State Bar investigation reported that the attorney had relationships at multiple organizational levels and, at times, provided meals, gifts, parties, private plane travel, and other benefits to State Bar personnel while his disciplinary matters were pending.[15]

During my first year of law school, I successfully appealed a family law case *pro se* by demonstrating that the trial court had miscalculated child support. In my second year, I filed a complaint against a judge for making a biased statement that was not reflected in the record. As an attorney, I continued to advocate for justice by volunteering as a fee arbitrator, representing domestic violence survivors pro bono, and handling legal malpractice cases.

I trusted the legal system and believed I could eventually resolve the issues arising from the State Bar's case. Unfortunately, I underestimated the severity of the situation.

CRIMINAL CHARGES

The following illustrates how unresolved fee issues can evolve into consequences far beyond billing disagreements.

The criminal charges were based on the State Bar's disciplinary trial, in which the prosecutor engaged in actions that, in my view, raised ethical and procedural concerns. I believe that if I had been represented by an experienced bar defense attorney, numerous issues could have been properly addressed. The court may have given greater consideration to these matters with knowledgeable counsel involved.

I received notice of the criminal charges by mail and was not arrested or taken into custody. The charges included a lengthy list of allegations with a potential 20-year prison sentence. There were charges that lacked a factual basis, suggesting they were made without adequate supporting evidence. Criminal prosecutions should rely on credible proof, not on unsubstantiated claims.[16]

Once I received the criminal charges, it became clear that my problems were far more serious than I had imagined, as my liberty was indeed in jeopardy. During my first meeting with a criminal attorney, he outlined several possible defense motions, which led me to borrow a significant amount for his retainer. However, the motions were never filed. And it was only during my attempt to appeal the trial court's ruling that I uncovered issues with the credibility of the charges.

After several months of pretrial proceedings, my criminal attorney called one afternoon and gave me an hour to decide whether to proceed to trial or accept a negotiated plea. I had one hour to make a life-altering decision.

I relied on what I now believe to be inaccurate and incomplete information and entered into a plea deal. I requested specific language in the plea bargain to clarify that I failed to include relevant terms in the fee agreement because I relied on a client's verbal promises.

PLEA BARGAIN

Our justice system handles an overwhelming volume of criminal cases. While the Sixth Amendment of the U.S. Constitution guarantees a right "...to a speedy and public trial," 97% of federal and 94% of state convictions result from guilty pleas.[17]

Legal scholars quoted in a Supreme Court opinion have stated that plea bargaining "...is not some adjunct to the criminal justice system; it is the criminal justice system."[18]

U.S. District Judge Jed S. Rakoff discussed the problem with plea bargains: "In actuality, our criminal justice system is almost exclusively a system of plea bargaining, negotiated behind closed doors and with no judicial oversight. The outcome is very largely determined by the prosecutor alone."[19]

If I had been found guilty of all the criminal allegations listed in the original complaint, it could have resulted in 20 years in prison. Yet the actual outcome of my plea bargain was a possible six months in county jail, with the judge deciding whether that was even necessary. So, the question is, if the charges were so serious, how is it that 20 years were whittled down to six months?

Were the prosecutors inept at negotiating, or was my criminal attorney exceptionally skilled? Neither is correct. The purpose of the plea-bargaining system is to terrify defendants into settling their cases. Although the Sixth Amendment guarantees the right to a speedy and public trial, our current system relies heavily on plea bargains and often discourages actual trials. While the substantive issues surrounding plea agreements in criminal cases are beyond the scope of this book, it is well known that cost-effective plea bargains are a preferred alternative to expensive and time-consuming trials. But what do we lose as a consequence?

The magnitude of the criminal charges had the practical effect of pressuring me to accept a plea. I was scared and overwhelmed, knowing that my limited resources and the likelihood of an overburdened public defender left me with little hope for justice. As a result, I resigned myself to accepting the alternative.

Before sentencing, I met with the probation officer who would recommend the length of my sentence, if any. Unfortunately, he only received documents from the District Attorney because my statements and supporting information were never submitted to him. I believe this prevented the probation officer from fully understanding the facts of my case.

Subsequently, at the final hearing, based on the probation officer's recommendations, I was sentenced to one year in jail. My sentence was then immediately reduced to six months due to recent regulations regarding overcrowding. Although I received the original notice of the charges against me by mail, I was handcuffed, immediately led out of the courtroom, and transported to jail without any opportunity to settle my affairs.

INCARCERATION

As I walked out of the courtroom in handcuffs, the grim reality of my situation sank in. I spent the next 24 hours in the jail attached to the courthouse. I wore the same suit I had worn to trial and slept on a hard bench. Several times during my brief stay, I was given sandwiches in a paper bag. The next day, I was transported to Las Colinas Women's Jail and placed in a dormitory-like building to find my way.

My criminal attorney never visited me in jail or offered any guidance to help me navigate those first terrifying days. Instead, our building's housemother, a self-proclaimed drug dealer, provided me with advice. For the first month, she was my primary source of information on how to get along, what to do, and what to avoid. An avid Scrabble player, she won nine out of every ten games we played. I survived that first month in the general population mainly due to her kindness. The following month, I transferred to the trustee building, where conditions were somewhat more tolerable. As trustees, we had slightly more leeway and better conditions because we worked every day sewing inmate uniforms.

Sitting on my bunk that first month, I had plenty of time to reflect on the events that led to my current situation. Had I expected too much from my criminal attorney, or could he have done more to help? How did the State Bar's decision for disbarment turn into criminal allegations that could lead to 20 years in prison?

Jail has been called a time-out for adults. Well, I used that time to focus on my rights, which I believed had been denied. For the past eight years, I had been a legal advocate for those who could not afford legal representation and for domestic violence survivors like myself, whose credibility was often questioned. I worked extremely hard to protect their rights. Yet here I was, in jail after a rush to judgment that ignored the laws and principles I had previously fought to uphold.

DENIAL OF ACCESS TO A LAW LIBRARY

I quickly realized that I needed to file several legal motions to contest my plea, as I believed I had received inaccurate information and inadequate legal representation. My criminal attorney failed to challenge several issues as promised, and in hindsight, I believe critical aspects of my defense were overlooked. Although his retainer was substantial, the time he devoted to my case did not seem proportional. As the disbarment order had not yet been finalized, I still had the opportunity to petition the Supreme Court of California to review the State Bar proceedings and potentially overturn the State Bar's ruling.

Subsequent developments became interesting, but not in a positive way. During the first few days of my incarceration, I asked for and received a law library pass several times to research my options. The "law library" was a small room with a limited-access computer and a few codebooks. However, the very next week, my request for a library pass was denied. When I asked a guard why I couldn't gain access, she told me the law library had closed. When I asked my jail counselor, she claimed she would schedule library time for me, an assertion that was nonsensical because the library had already been shut down. She seemed unaware of the closure. In fact, the jail locked down the law library just *one week* after I began my sentence, which denied me access to the resources I needed to address my legal issues.

I had legitimate concerns about my sentence, given that two local cases with far more egregious charges resulted in no jail time for either party. I later discovered that "a bargained-for sentence that substantially exceeds the norm for the crime is probably due to some kind of defense attorney mistake."[20] However, my efforts to address this and other issues were blocked once the law library doors were slammed shut.

I will never know whether the library's closure was just a coincidence or an intentional act to prevent a former attorney from accessing legal resources. Afterward, I filed several grievances within the jail, describing the absence of a law library. I never received a response. Both the U.S. Department of Justice and the State of California require comprehensive written policies and procedures to ensure that all incarcerated individuals have the opportunity to submit and appeal grievances regarding their conditions of confinement.[21]

Yet, it appears that such requirements can be disregarded without consequence. I certainly could not afford to retain another attorney, so I was unable to file a habeas petition when access to the law library was denied.

The closure of the law library also prevented me from petitioning the California Supreme Court to review the errors from the State Bar trial. With no legal resources available, I relied on the only accessible tools I had: a golf pencil and a pad of paper. I sent a handwritten letter to the Supreme Court of California, explaining that I could not file a petition due to the nonexistent law library.

In response, I received a letter from the Supreme Court clerk stating they would not accept my handwritten petition. The deadline for filing for relief from the State Bar's ruling expired while I was incarcerated.

CONSTITUTIONAL RIGHTS: GUARANTEED FOR ALL OR RESERVED FOR THOSE WHO CAN PAY?

The repetition of errors in my case created a never-ending pattern: I was unable to secure counsel for the State Bar trial, endured questionable representation from my criminal attorney, denied access to a law library, received no response to my jail grievances and the California Supreme Court refused to accept my handwritten request for relief. The ignoble adherence to the finality doctrine shattered my faith in the system and left me in disbelief. After serving five and a half months in jail, I was released, but with a felony conviction that made even finding a minimum-wage job impossible. Desperate to make sense of everything that had happened, I began researching possible avenues for recourse.

I filed a civil action under 42 U.S.C. Section 1983 seeking relief for violations of my First, Sixth, and Fourteenth Amendment rights. For three years, I pursued an appeal, but ultimately I was unsuccessful because the court concluded that I had not suffered any injury because I had not filed a habeas petition. It didn't seem to matter that I was effectively prevented from doing so due to a lack of access to a law library or even a meaningful alternative. This circular reasoning was deeply disheartening.

I was also precluded from pursuing a legal malpractice claim against my criminal attorney. Because I was denied access to a law library while incarcerated, I could not file for post-conviction relief, a legal prerequisite to bringing such a claim. In effect, I was prevented from challenging my conviction and holding my attorney accountable. "Post conviction exoneration is a prerequisite to prevailing on a legal malpractice claim."[22] Without a path forward, my sense of injustice was compounded.

The late U.S. Supreme Court Justice Ruth Bader Ginsburg reaffirmed our nation's commitment to justice by referencing the inscription above the entrance to the U.S. Supreme Court: "Equal Justice Under Law." Although she also stated, "It remains true, however, that the poor, and even the middle class, encounter financial impediments to a day in court. They do not enjoy the secure access available to those with full purses or political muscle."[23]

Professor Erwin Chemerinsky authored the book, *Closing the Court House Door.*[24] He writes that the U.S. Supreme Court's decisions over the past ten years have been "almost uniformly hostile to the enforcement of individual citizens' constitutional rights." He describes the difficulty injured parties face in accessing federal courts. He believes the courts should be available to all who claim a violation of their constitutional rights, not just in cases of political appeal. His book illustrates how easily an individual's constitutional rights can be disregarded.

The above quotations express valid concerns regarding an individual's right to their day in court. From my experience, I have learned that when access to the justice system is blocked, intentionally ignored, or prohibitively expensive, constitutional protections are eroded with little regard for the lasting consequences.

Attorney fees play a critical role in an individual's access to justice. The act of questioning and challenging unreasonable fees is a meaningful step toward an equitable system. Change can only begin when we refuse to accept the results of a flawed process. "There can be no equal justice where the kind of trial a man gets depends on the amount of money he has."[25]

Although I can no longer practice law or provide legal advice, I can share what I've learned to help litigants better understand their legal fees. In addition to a legal background, I have years of experience teaching finance at both the undergraduate and graduate levels and spent the last decade researching legal fee issues. I created this guide to make a complicated and intimidating subject easier to navigate. In addition, the website www.attorneyfeehustle.com is available to provide real answers (not AI) to readers' questions.

CONCLUSION

Education is the most effective way to prevent unreasonable attorney fees. By learning how to recognize unfair billing practices, you can identify problematic charges early, ask informed questions, and challenge excessive fees before they become overwhelming.

My goal is to demystify bill-padding practices and simplify the process of disputing unreasonable fees. Drawing on years of research, this guide offers clear, practical steps to help you evaluate problematic legal bills with confidence and address questionable charges effectively.

Currently, contesting attorney fees can be a daunting process, largely regulated, managed, and overseen by attorneys. To pursue a lawsuit against your attorney for excessive billing, you may need to retain another attorney, hire an expert to evaluate the disputed fees, and pay court costs and other litigation expenses—all to challenge charges that may have been unethical from the start.

It is important to understand that the legal profession is a self-regulating body that manages its own ethical obligations to act in the public interest. Because of this type of governance, the burden should be on the legal profession to establish an equitable system for addressing unethical fees. Even free mediation or arbitration services can favor attorneys over clients who represent themselves. Attorneys who charge unreasonable fees should be held accountable without imposing additional costs on their clients.

If you cannot resolve a fee dispute directly with your attorney, filing a misconduct complaint with the state bar may be a viable option. This guide will help you take that step. When attorneys fail to uphold their fiduciary and ethical obligations regarding legal fees, clients may have access to a no-cost process to challenge excessive charges, though persistence may be required. Remember, you have the right to a transparent disclosure of the legal fees charged in your case. The information in this book will help you protect that right and avoid the Attorney Fee Hu$tle.

---

1. American Bar Association, *Resolution 112A*, 2006.
2. Bowers, Josh and Robinson, Paul, "Perceptions of Fairness and Justice: The Shared Aims and Occasional Conflicts of Legitimacy and Moral Credibility," *Wake Forest Law Review* 47 (2012): 215–216; Rosales-Mireles v. United States, 138 S. Ct. 1897 (2018).
3. Ginsburg, Ruth Bader, "In Pursuit of the Public Good: Access to Justice in the United States," *Washington University Journal of Law & Policy* 7, no. 1 (2001): 1–15.
4. American Bar Association, "Rule 1.5: Fees," in *Model Rules of Professional Conduct,* 2020.
5. *Bass v. Rose*, 609 SE 2d 848 – W Va:(Supreme Court of Appeals 2024).
6. American Bar Association, "Preamble and Scope" in *Model Rules of Professional Conduct,* 2020.
7. Levin, Leslie C. "The Ethical World of Solo and Small Law Firm Practitioners," 41 *Hous. L.Rev.* 309, 312–13 (2004).

8. Hansen, Mark, "Picking on the Little Guy: Perception Lingers That Discipline Falls Hardest on Solos, Small Firms," *ABA Journal* 89, no. 3 (2003): 30–34.

9. The State Bar of California, "Open Letter Regarding the State Bar's Thomas V. Girardi Disclosure," Open-Letter-Girardi-Disclosure-11-03-22PDF.

10. Halpern, May, Ybarra, Gelber, Independent Investigation for the State Bar of California: Report of Investigation, February 4, 2023.

11. "Our Mission: What We Do," The State Bar of California.

12. *Walker v. State Bar*, 49 Cal.3d 1107 (Cal. 1989).

13. ABA Model Rule 34, Model Rules for Lawyer Disciplinary Enforcement.

14. *Walker v. State Bar*, 49 Cal.3d 1107 (Cal. 1989).

15. Halpern, May, Ybarra, Gelber, Independent Investigation for the State Bar of California: Report of Investigation, February 4, 2023.

16. *Addison v. State of California*, 21 Cal.3d 313, 146 Cal. Rptr. 224, 578 P.2d 941 (Cal. 1978).

17. U.S. Dept. of Justice, United States Attorneys' Annual Statistical Report Fiscal Year 2023, Table 2A. fy2023-cover-intro-toc-tablesPDF

18. Scott, Robert E., and Stuntz, William J., "Plea Bargaining as Contract," *The Yale Law Journal* 101, no. 8 (1992): 1909–68, quoted in Missouri v. Frye, 132 S. Ct. 1399 (2012).

19. Rakoff, Jed S., *Why The Innocent Plead Guilty And The Guilty Go Free* (New York: Farrar, Straus and Giroux, 2021).

20. Robert E. Scott and William J. Stuntz, "Plea Bargaining as Contract," *The Yale Law Journal* 101, no. 8 (1992): 1909–68.

21. United States Code of Federal Regulation Title 28 Chapter I Part 40 Amended 1/17/2025. 15 Cal. Code. Regs. § 1073.

22. *Coscia v. McKenna Cuneo,* 25 P.3d 670 (Cal. 2001).

23. Ginsburg, "In Pursuit of the Public Good."

24. Chemerinsky, Erwin, *Closing the Courthouse Door: How Your Constitutional Rights Became Unenforceable* (New Haven: Yale University Press, 2017).

25. *Griffin v. Illinois,* 351 U.S. 12 (1956).

WORKS CITED

A

Addison v. State of California, 21 Cal.3d 313, 146 Cal. Rptr. 224, 578 P.2d 941 (Cal. 1978).

American Bar Association, "Current ABA Definition of Paralegal,"

American Bar Association, "Demographics," in *ABA Profile of the Legal Profession 2023*, 2023.

American Bar Association, "Model Rules for Lawyer Disciplinary Enforcement. Rule 34."

American Bar Association, "Rule 1.5: Fees," in Model Rules of Professional Conduct, 2020.

American Bar Association, "Rule 1.8 art i.: Current Clients: Specific Rules," in Model Rules of Professional Conduct, 2020.

American Bar Association, "Rule 8.4: Misconduct" in Model Rules of Professional Conduct, 2020.

American Bar Association, "Preamble and Scope," in *Model Rules of Professional Conduct*, 2020.

American Bar Association, *Resolution 112A*, 2006.

American Bar Association Standing Committee on Ethics and Professional Responsibility, *Billing for Professional Fees, Disbursement Disbursements and Other Expenses*, Formal Opinion 93-379, 1993.

American Bar Association, Standing Committee on Ethics and Professional Responsibility, Formal Opinion 505,

American Bar Association Standing Committee on Paralegals, *ABA Model Guidelines for the Utilization of Paralegal Services* (Chicago, Illinois: American Bar Association, 2018).

American Bar Association Unbundling Resource Center.

Ariely, Dan *The (Honest) Truth about Dishonesty: How We Lie to Everyone--Especially Ourselves* (New York: Harper Perennial, 2013).

Attorney Grievance Commission v. Gregory Wayne Jones, AG No.: 1, September Term 2021.

B

Balducci v. Cige, 240 N.J. 574,592 (N.J. 2020).

Banks v. Dudek, Dist. Court, WD Kentucky 2025.

Bass v. Rose, 609 SE 2d 848 – W Va: (Supreme Court of Appeals 2004).

Beaver, Dennis H. Esq., "Overbilled by Your Lawyer? You're Not Alone" *Kiplinger Newsletter,* January 9, 2024.

Bieber, Christy, "How Much Do Lawyers Cost? 2023 Guide," *Forbes,* July 18, 2023.

Bilazzo v. Portfolio Recovery Associates, LLC, 876 F. Supp. 2d 452 (D.N.J. 2012).

Bird v. Superior Court, 130 Cal. Rptr. 2d 782 (Cal. Ct. App. 2003).

Board Of Professional Responsibility, Wyoming State v. Casper, 318 P. 3d 790 - Wyo: Supreme Court 2014.

Boothe-Perry, Nicola A. "No Laughing Matter: The Intersection of Legal Malpractice and Professionalism." *American University Journal of Gender Social Policy and Law* 21, no. 1 (2012): 1-37.

Bowers, Josh and Robinson, Paul, "Perceptions of Fairness and Justice: The Shared Aims and Occasional Conflicts of Legitimacy and Moral Credibility," *Wake Forest Law Review* 47 (2012): 215–216; Rosales-Mireles v. United States, 138 S. Ct. 1897 (2018).

Brandt v. Astrue, 2009 WL 1727472, at *4 (D. Or. June 16, 2009).

Bratton v. Thomas Law Firm, PC, 943 F. Supp. 2d 897 (N.D. Ind. 2013).

Britannica.com 2025 dictionary. Accessed Feb. 17, 2025.

Jean de la Bruyere, 17th century French philosopher.

C

In re C.L.W., 2024-Ohio-1519, 2024 WL 1714504, ¶ 59 (12th Dist.).

State Bar of California, "Analysis of Potential Bill Padding and Other Billing Issues", *Arbitration Advisory* 2016-02, 2016.

The State Bar of California, "Complaints & Claims."

The State Bar of California, "Open Letter Regarding the State Bar's Thomas V. Girardi Disclosure,"
Open-Letter-Girardi-Disclosure-11-03-22PDF.

The State Bar of California Standing Committee on Professional Responsibility and Conduct. *Arbitration Advisory* no. 2025-01.

The State Bar of California, "Determination of a "Reasonable" Fee," *Arbitration Advisory* 1998-03, updated March 20, 2015.

The State Bar of California, "Our Mission: What We Do."

In re C.L.W., 2024-Ohio-1519.
In re Campbell, 140 BR 35 - Bankr. Court, ED New York 1992 140 B.R. 35 (1992).
Charles v. LeBlanc, Dist. Court, WD Louisiana 2025, Civil Action No. 18-0541.
Chemerinsky, Erwin, *Closing the Courthouse Door: How Your Constitutional Rights Became Unenforceable* (New Haven: Yale University Press, 2017).
Chen, Vivia, "The US Overbilling Scandal: Why We Should Not Be So Shocked," *Law.Com International,* January 24, 2019.
Chin, Gabriel, J. and Wells, Scott C., "Can a Reasonable Doubt Have an Unreasonable Price? Limitations on Attorneys' Fee in Criminal Cases," *Boston College Law Review* 41, no. 1 (December 1, 2000): 1–70.
Clemens v. N.Y. Cent. Mut. Fire Ins. Co., 903 F.3d 396 (3d Cir. 2018).
Clio. *2023 Legal Trends Report.* 2023.
Cobb v. City of Roswell, Ga, 987 F. Supp. 2d 1319 (N.D. Ga. 2013).
Cobell v. Norton, 407 F. Supp. 2d 140 (D.D.C. 2005).
Coscia v. McKenna Cuneo, 25 P.3d 670 (Cal. 2001).
Colorado Supreme Court, Office of Attorney Regulation Counsel, "Complaints/Discipline–FAQs," Accessed April 2, 2024.
Copeland v. Marshall, 641 F.2d 880 (D.C. Cir. 1980).
Court Listener.

D

Davis v. City & County of San Francisco, 976 F.2d 1536, 1543 (9th Cir 1992) (citing *Missouri v. Jenkins,* 491 U.S. 274, (1989).
In re Dawson, 8 P.3d 856, 860 (N.M. 2000).

Diment, Dmitry, *Family Law & Divorce Lawyers & Attorneys in the US,* IBISWorld. November 2024.
Dobbs v. DePuy Orthopedics, Inc., 842 F.3d 1045 (7th Cir. 2016).
Dowling v. Chicago Options Associates, Inc., 875 NE 2d 1012 - Ill: Supreme Court 2007.

E

El Apple I, Ltd. v. Olivas, 370 SW 3d 757 - Tex: (Supreme Court 2012).

F

Fierros v. Quebedeaux Buick GMC Inc., No. CV-20-00245-TUC-RM (MSA) (D. Ariz. 2021).
Fralick v. Plumbers & Pipefitters Nat'l Pension Fund, 2011 WL 487754 (N.D. Tex. 2011).
"File a Grievance," State Bar of Texas, accessed April 2, 2024.
The Florida Bar v. Moriber, 314 So.2d 145, 148 (Fla.1975).
Francis v. Atl. Infiniti, Ltd., 2012 N.Y. Slip Op. 50198 (N.Y. Sup. Ct. 2012).

G

Matter of Gendel, 303 A. 3d 1292, 255 NJ 500 (NJ: Supreme Court, 2023).
Disciplinary Proceedings Against Gillette, 895 NW 2d 1 - Wis: Supreme Court 2017.
George v. GTE Directories Corp., 114 F. Supp. 2d 1281 (M.D. Fla. 2000).

K. William Gibson, ed., *Flying Solo: A Survival Guide for the Solo and Small Firm Lawyer*, 4th ed. (Chicago, Illinois: ABA Law Practice Division, 2014).

Gill Sav. Ass'n v. Int'l Supply Co., 759 S.W.2d 697, 702 (Tex. App.-Dallas. 1988, writ denied).

Ginsburg, Ruth Bader, "In Pursuit of the Public Good: Access to Justice in the United States," *Washington University Journal of Law & Policy* 7, no. 1 (2001): 1–15.

Goldfarb v. Virginia State Bar, 421 U.S. 773 (1975).

Griffin v. Illinois, 351 U.S. 12 (1956).

Guidry v. Clare, 442 F. Supp. 2d 282 (E.D. Va. 2006).

Gurule v. Land Guardian, Inc., 912 F.3d 252 (5th Cir. 2018).

H

Halpern, May, Ybarra, Gelber, Independent Investigation for the State Bar of California: Report of Investigation, February 4, 2023.

Hansen, Mark, "Picking on the Little Guy: Perception Lingers That Discipline Falls Hardest on Solos, Small Firms," *ABA Journal* 89, no. 3 (2003): 30–34.

Law Off. Of Mark S. Helweil v. Karambelas, 2019 NY Slip Op 32308 - NY: Supreme Court 2019.

Hensley v. Eckerhart, 461 U.S. 424 (1983).

Hernandez v. Saybrook Buick GMC, Inc., No. 3:20-cv-00438 (VAB) (D. Conn. 2021).

Holladay v. Gestamp, LLC, Dist. Court, ND Alabama 2025.

J

J.G. v. NYC Department of Education, 23 Civ. 959 (SDNY 2024).
In Re Johnson, 317 B.R. 347 (Bankr. C.D. Ill. 2004).
Johnson, Laura et al., "Establishing Best Billing Practices Through Billing Guidelines: Fostering Trust and Transparency on Legal Costs," *University of Arkansas at Little Rock Law Review* 39, no. 1 (2016): 1–24.

K

Keith v. Volpe, 644 F.Supp. 1312, 1316 (C.D.Cal. 1986).
Key Bank National Ass'n v. Van Noy, 598 F. Supp. 2d 1160 (D. Or. 2009).
Koontz v. Wells Fargo NA, Dist. Court, SD West Virginia 2013.
Kreamer v. Town of Oxford, 96 A.D.3d 1128, 946 N.Y.S.2d 283, 2012 N.Y. Slip Op. 4445 (N.Y. App. Div. 2012).
In re Kutner, 78 Ill.2d 157, 35 Ill.Dec. 674, 399 N.E.2d 963, 966 (1979) (quoting *The Florida Bar v. Moriber,* 314 So.2d 145, 148 (Fla.1975)).

L

Lerman, Lisa, "Lying to Clients," *University of Pennsylvania Law Review* 138 (1990): 659–760.
Lerman, Lisa, "Regulation of Unethical Billing Practices: Progress and Prospects," *The Professional Lawyer,* 1998, 90–97.
Levin, Leslie C. "The Ethical World of Solo and Small Law Firm Practitioners," 41 *Hous. L.Rev.* 309, 312–13 (2004).
Levin, Leslie and Robbennolt, Jennifer K., "To Err is Human, To Apologize is Hard: The Role of Apologies in Lawyer

Discipline" (2021). *Faculty Articles and Papers. 578.*
Lewallen v. City of Beaumont, Dist. Court, ED Texas 2009.
Lilly v. City of New York, 934 F. 3d 222 - Court of Appeals, 2nd Circuit 2019.
Lucas V. Hamm, 56 Cal.2 583, (CA Supreme Court 1961).
LV v. New York City Dept. of Educ., 700 F. Supp. 2d 510 (S.D.N.Y. 2010).

M

Marsh v. Digital Equipment Corp., 699 F. Supp. 1411 (D. Ariz. 1988).
Mattson, 2002 S.D. 112, ¶ 55, 651 N.W.2d at 289 (quoting *In re Discipline of Tidball,* 503 N.W.2d 850, 856 (S.D. 1993)).
McMackin v. McMackin, 651 A.2d 778 (Del. Fam. 1993).
Merrick v. Scott, Dist. Court, ND (Texas 2011).
Miller v. Alamo, 983 F.2d 856, 862 (8th Cir. 1993).
Missouri v. Jenkins, 491 U.S. 274 (1989).
Morris v. Belfor USA Group, Inc., 201 P. 3d 1253 - Colo: Court of Appeals, 7th Div. 2008.

N

Nadarajah v. Holder, 569 F. 3d 906 (9th Cir. 2009).
The National Federation of Paralegal Associations, *Model Code of Ethics and Professional Responsibility* (The National Federation of Paralegal Associations, 2016).
North Coast Electric Co. v. Selig, 151 P. 3d 211 (Wash. Ct. App. 2007).
Matter of Navis Realty, Inc., 126 B.R. 137 (Bankr. E.D.N.Y. 1991).

O

In re Olson, 884 F.2d 1415, 1428 (D.C. Cir. 1989).

In re Orthopaedic Technology, Inc., 97 B.R. 596 (Bankr. D. Colo. 1989).

P

Dan Packel, "Lawyers Caught Overbilling? The Billable Hour Shares the Blame," *The American Lawyer,* January 18, 2019.

Perez v. Kirk Carrigan, 822 S.W.2d 261, 265 (Tex. App.—Corpus Christi 1991, writ denied).

"Preparing for a Mediation," United States Court of Appeals for the Fourth Circuit, accessed February 1, 2025. Disclaimer: The permitted use of this quotation does not constitute an endorsement of the book or its contents by the judiciary or the court.

Precision Seed Cleaners v. Country Mut. Ins. Co., 976 F. Supp. 2d 1228 (D. Or. 2013).

R

Rakoff, Jed S., *Why The Innocent Plead Guilty And The Guilty Go Free* (New York: Farrar, Straus and Giroux, 2021).

Ramos, Manual, "Legal Malpractice: The Profession's Dirty Little Secret," *Vanderbilt Law Review* 47, no. 6 (1994): 1657.

Richmond, Douglas R., "For a Few Dollars More: The Perplexing Problem of Unethical Billing Practices by Lawyers," *South Carolina Law Review* 60, no. 1 (2008): 63–121.

Darlene Ricker, "Greed, Ignorance, and Overbilling: Some Lawyers Have Given New Meaning to the Term 'Legal Fiction,'" *ABA Journal* 80, no. 8 (1994): 62–66.
Ridgeway v. Wal-Mart Stores Inc., 269 F. Supp. 3d 975, 991 (N.D. Cal. 2017).*Role Models America, Inc. v. Brownlee,* 353 F.3d 962 (D.C. Cir. 2004).
In re Romansky, 938 A.2d 733,743 (D.C. 2007).
William G. Ross, *The Honest Hour: The Ethics of Time-Based Billing by Attorneys* (Durham, N.C: Carolina Academic Press, 1996).

S

Salton Bay Marina, Inc. v. Imperial Irrigation Dist., 172 Cal.App.3d 914, 951 (Cal. Ct. App. 1985).
Schachner, Robert W. and Phillips, John, *How & When to Sue Your Lawyer: What You Need to Know* (Garden City Park, N.Y: Square One Publishers, 2005).
Schlenker v. Cascino, 2012 NY Slip Op 33066 - NY: Supreme Court, Albany 2012.
Scott, Robert E., and Stuntz, William J., "Plea Bargaining as Contract," *The Yale Law Journal* 101, no. 8 (1992): 1909–68, quoted in *Missouri v. Frye,* 132 S. Ct. 1399 (2012).
Shaw v. Silver, 95 AD 3d 416 - NY: Appellate Div., 1st Dept. 2012.
Disciplinary Proceedings Against Siderits, 824 NW 2d 812 - Wis: Supreme Court 2013.
Simon, Roy (1994) "Gross Profits? An Introduction to a Program on Legal Fees," *Hofstra Law Review*: Vol. 22 : Iss. 3 , Article 2.
State Dept. of Transp. v. Skidmore, 720 So. 2d 1125 (Fla. Dist. Ct. App. 1998).

Swisher v. U.S., 262 F. Supp. 2d 1203 (D. Kan. 2003).
Spegon v. Catholic Bishop of Chicago, 175 F.3d 544 (7th Cir. 1999).

T

Taylor v. Chubb Group of Ins. Companies, 874 P.2d 806 (Okla. 1994).
Taylor v. District of Columbia, 325 F. Supp. 144 (D.D.C. 2018).
In re Teligent, Inc., 640 F.3d 53, 57-58 (2d Cir. 2011).
Tobin v. Gordon, 614 F. Supp. 2d 514 - Dist. Court, D. (Delaware 2009).

U

Ursic v. Bethlehem Mines, 719 F.2d 670 (3d Cir. 1983).
U. Slate, Tile Composition v. G M Roofing, 732 F.2d 495, 502 n. 2 (6th Cir. 1984).
U.S. v. Genova, 167 F. Supp. 2d 1021 - Dist. Court, ND Illinois 2001167 F.Supp.2d 1021 (2001).
United States Code of Federal Regulation Title 28 Chapter I Part 40 Amended 1/17/2025. 15 Cal. Code. Regs. § 1073.
U.S. Dept. of Justice, United States Attorneys' Annual Statistical Report Fiscal Year 2023, Table 2A. fy2023-cover-intro-toc-tablesPDF.
U.S. Bureau of Labor Statistics, "Occupational Employment and Wage Statistics: Paralegals and Legal Assistants," April 25, 2023.

W

Walker v. State Bar, 49 Cal.3d 1107 (Cal. 1989).
Weiss, Debra Cassens, "Red-Flag Billing Practices Chronicled; Report Finds 'upbilling' by 21 Percent of Law Firms." *ABA Journal*, March 28, 2017.
Weiss, Debra Cassens, "Lawyer Accused of Billing over 24 Hours in a Day Suspended; but Official Said Others Were Worse," *ABA Journal*, April 26, 2017.
Committee on Legal Ethics of W. Va. State Bar v. Tatterson, 352 S.E.2d 107, 113 (W. Va. 1986).
Wisconsin Court System, "Lawyer Regulation," accessed April 2, 2024.
World Justice Project, "Global Scores & Rankings."

Y

Young v. Spencer, 405 P.3d 701 (Okla. Civ. App. 2017).

INDEX

A

B

E

F

L

M

N

O

P

www.ingramcontent.com/pod-product-compliance
Lightning Source LLC
LaVergne TN
LVHW050812061126
851857LV00012B/770
9798218833732